T0320908

Macroeconomic Inequality from Reagan to Trump

For five decades, rising US income and wealth inequality has been driven by wage repression and production realignments benefitting the top one percent of households. In this inaugural book for Cambridge Studies in New Economic Thinking, Professor Lance Taylor takes an innovative approach to measuring inequality, providing the first and only full integration of distributional and macro level data for the US. While work by Thomas Piketty and colleagues pursues integration from the income side, Professor Taylor uses data of distributions by size of income and wealth combined with the cost and demand sides, flows of funds, and full balance sheet accounting of real capital and financial claims. This blends measures of inequality with national income and product accounts to show the relationship between productivity and wages at the industry sector level. Taylor assesses the scope and nature of various interventions to reduce income and wealth inequalities using his simulation model, disentangling wage growth and productivity while challenging mainstream models.

LANCE TAYLOR is the Arnhold Professor Emeritus of International Cooperation and Development and was director of the Center for Economic Policy Analysis at the New School for Social Research.

Studies in New Economic Thinking

The 2008 financial crisis pointed to problems in economic theory that require more than just big data to solve. INET's series in New Economic Thinking exists to ensure that innovative work that advances economics and better integrates it with other social sciences and the study of history and institutions can reach a broad audience in a timely way.

Macroeconomic Inequality from Reagan to Trump

Market Power, Wage Repression, Asset Price Inflation, and Industrial Decline

LANCE TAYLOR

New School for Social Research, New York
(with contributions from Özlem Ömer)

CAMBRIDGE
UNIVERSITY PRESS

CAMBRIDGE
UNIVERSITY PRESS

University Printing House, Cambridge CB2 8BS, United Kingdom

One Liberty Plaza, 20th Floor, New York, NY 10006, USA

477 Williamstown Road, Port Melbourne, VIC 3207, Australia

314–321, 3rd Floor, Plot 3, Splendor Forum, Jasola District Centre, New Delhi – 110025, India

79 Anson Road, #06–04/06, Singapore 079906

Cambridge University Press is part of the University of Cambridge.

It furthers the University's mission by disseminating knowledge in the pursuit of education, learning, and research at the highest international levels of excellence.

www.cambridge.org
Information on this title: www.cambridge.org/9781108494632
DOI: 10.1017/9781108854443

First published 2020

A catalogue record for this publication is available from the British Library.

Library of Congress Cataloging-in-Publication Data
Names: Taylor, Lance, 1940– author.
Title: Macroeconomic inequality from Reagan to Trump : market power, wage repression, asset price inflation, and industrial decline / Lance Taylor, New School for Social Research, New York, with contributions from Özlem Ömer.
Description: Cambridge, United Kingdom ; New York, NY : Cambridge University Press, 2020. | Series: Studies in new economic thinking | Includes bibliographical references and index.
Identifiers: LCCN 2019057853 (print) | LCCN 2019057854 (ebook) | ISBN 9781108494632 (hardback) | ISBN 9781108854443 (ebook)
Subjects: LCSH: Income distribution – United States – History – 20th century. | Income distribution – United States – History – 21st century. | Macroeconomics – United States – History – 20th century. | Macroeconomics – United States – History – 21st century. | United States – Economic conditions – 1945–
Classification: LCC HC110.I5 T39 2020 (print) | LCC HC110.I5 (ebook) | DDC 339.20973–dc23
LC record available at https://lccn.loc.gov/2019057853
LC ebook record available at https://lccn.loc.gov/2019057854

ISBN 978-1-108-49463-2 Hardback
ISBN 978-1-108-79610-1 Paperback

Contents

Figures

Tables

Acknowledgments

The Institute for New Economic Thinking (INET) generously supported the work that went into this book through a series of grants to the Schwartz Center for Economic Policy Analysis at the New School for Social Research. Duncan Foley, Nelson Barbosa, Armon Rezai, Thomas Ferguson, and three referees provided numerous comments (most heeded, some not). Barbosa took the lead in restating the NIPA accounts in the form of a SAM. The heavy lifting was done by New School grad students including Rezai, Laura Carvalho, Rishabh Kumar, and especially Özlem Ömer who made major contributions to Chapters 4 and 6. I am grateful to them all, to the staff of the Schwartz Center and the New School Department of Economics, and to Thomas Ferguson at INET.

Introduction

This book is about the macroeconomics of inequality in the USA, beginning around 1970. The analysis is based on a data framework combining the distributions by size of income and wealth with the income and output sides of the national accounts, flows of funds, and full balance-sheet accounting of real capital and financial claims. The numbers entering the household size distributions are mutually consistent and satisfy double-entry national accounting balances, making analysis and modeling roughly right about the big picture of distribution. The picture is "roughly right" because of the double-entry accounting consistency that goes into its creation.[1]

The first five chapters present the data, economic theory, and institutional analysis of fifty years of rising inequality. Chapter 6 sets out a numerical simulation model assessing future prospects for ameliorating the present distributive mess.

The key takeaway is that in the present-day American political economy, wage repression over decades is the basic cause of distributional malaise. "Big data" microeconomic detail is consistent with this finding but does not determine it – not monopoly power, not "superstar" firms. The model simulations show that undoing unequal distributions of income and wealth will take as much time as was needed to create them.

Wage repression operates through several channels, which will take some effort to trace. Here we first sketch the main observations coming from the data and simulation results. Because wages are central to the analysis, the discussion then turns to a preliminary analysis of the dynamics of payments to labor. We close this introduction with

---

[1] Other presentations such as Piketty et al. (2016) are less thorough because they consider only the income side of the national accounts.

a discussion of the broader political economy approach that animates the book as a whole and compare that with alternative perspectives.

FINDINGS FROM THE DATA

Chapters 1 through 5 suggest nine points about distributive shifts in the USA since around 1980.

Income and wealth distributions became substantially more unequal over a period of decades; "cumulative processes" of economic change were involved.

The profit share of output rose substantially. The wage share correspondingly went down; in accounting terms, because average real wage growth lagged rising labor productivity. Wage repression was the key driving force behind rising inequality. Increases in real labor compensation that actually occurred mostly flowed to the top 1 percent of households in the size distribution of income.

Workers have been pushed into low-wage, low-productivity sectors, contributing to an overall productivity slowdown. Both static and dynamic sectors have had lagging wage growth. Demand growth for manufacturing, information, and a few other dynamic sectors is offset by rising productivity so they shed labor although their wages are relatively high. Jobs trickle down to low-wage, low-productivity education–health, business service, and accommodation–food sectors with rising demand but slow productivity growth. A natural interpretation is that a productivity slowdown became a means to absorb surplus labor. Or, more baldly stated, business models changed to take advantage of the ever-growing masses of workers with no prospects for good jobs.

The top group of households also benefitted from interest and dividend payments supported by higher profits, together with rising proprietors' incomes. They received capital gains exceeding rising business profits after taxes and depreciation: via rising equity prices, companies effectively distributed more than they earned. Top 1 percent households also received "wages" including options and bonuses, and share buybacks. Because they have high saving rates, their net worth went up.

Higher capital gains were stimulated by wage repression in two ways. Businesses enjoyed rising profits and falling interest rates, the latter due to slower inflation because there was no wage-driven cost push. Insofar as asset price increases are driven by capitalization of higher profit rates as interest rates declined, they basically result from lagging wages.

Households at the bottom of the income distribution received modestly increasing government transfers. They apparently have negative saving rates, which supported their consumption spending.

Income of middle-class households, which principally rely on labor earnings, was squeezed from above and below; their share of total income went down.

Finally, summary measures underline the rapid growth of inequality. So-called Palma ratios that compare household incomes of the top 1 percent to incomes further down the scale increased by about 3 percent per year – an astonishingly high number for *any* macroeconomic ratio over a span of decades. The share of wealth in the total held by rich households was around 25 percent in the 1960s; now it is in the vicinity of 40 percent.

SIMULATION RESULTS

It is convenient to run simulations over a period of forty years, basically the span between Presidents Reagan and Trump. At a macro level over that time, visible realignment of the profit and wage shares would require steady growth of wages exceeding increases in productivity. A "double movement" of the type memorably chronicled by Karl Polanyi for the nineteenth century (as we will discuss) including institutional and social changes would certainly be necessary to allow labor to restore its income position. One-off policy moves such as tax and transfer packages in the range of $100 billion per year (half a percent of GDP) or minimum wage increases in the 10 to 20 percent range could knock a few points off Palma ratios, but would not alter the big picture of inequality.

Besides continued wage growth for the poor and middle classes, the rapid increases in labor payments to the top earners would have to be curtailed to push the Palmas down. Similar conclusions apply to financial transfers and proprietors' incomes flowing to the top 1 percent.

Growing government tax/transfer packages could benefit lower income groups. Resources could conceivably come from a wealth fund supported by taxes on capital gains. These taxes channeled to a wealth fund could halt increases in the share of wealth controlled by the top 1 percent.

Palma ratios and the 1 percent's wealth share could go down steadily if all these changes were to be combined.

These observations are robust insofar as they mainly build upon the accounting consistency underlying the simulation model. Policy is relevant only if it can support the distributional shifts built into the simulations.

PRODUCTIVITY AND WAGE REPRESSION

To unravel wage dynamics, it helps to bring in labor "productivity," a label economists use for the ratio of real output to employment. Productivity *is* just a ratio, but it is often interpreted as a measure of technical progress and assumed to have its own proper dynamics. Chapter 4 uses it to sort out changes in employment and output across producing sectors.

As explained in more detail in Chapter 4, the real "product wage" is the nominal or money wage divided by a producer price index – that is, corrected for cost inflation confronting business. A little algebra shows that the labor or wage share of output (which equals "unit labor cost") is equal to the real wage divided by productivity. Ignoring indirect taxes and government subsidies for producers for simplicity, the profit share equals 1 minus the wage share. Figure I.1 shows how the profit share and growth rates of real wages and productivity have varied over time. Real wage growth lagged productivity growth for almost 50 years after 1970, causing the profit share to

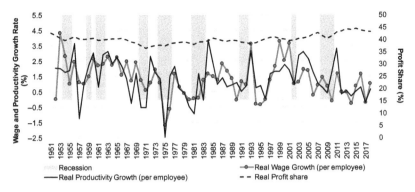

FIGURE I.I Real wage and productivity growth rates and profit share

grow at 0.43 percent per year, 1970–2018. Annual growth at a rate of 0.4 percent (= 0.004) looks tiny but over 50 years it cumulates to 27 percent. That's a big change for any income share! The real profit level grew at 3.2 percent per year vs 2.8 percent for real GDP

Weaker labor bargaining power after 1970 was a key factor. As discussed in Chapter 5, there is a cyclical pattern (which can be traced to Marx in the nineteenth century and the Cambridge economist Richard Goodwin in the twentieth) superimposed on the rising profit share. Except around 1995 and 2015, productivity growth led real wage growth as the economy emerged from recessions (shaded). Typically since 1970, productivity growth has been stronger. Subsequent wage growth and a dip in the profit share lead into a new recession.[2]

Figure I.2 illustrates the slowdown in inflation across business cycles. The lower diagram shows that, coming out of a recession, the growth rate of a producer price index tends to exceed the rise of nominal unit labor costs (money wage growth minus productivity growth) so the profit share increases as in Figure I.1. The pattern is reversed late in the cycle as the profit share tails off (subject to real

<hr />

[2]   A similar observation applies to the "yield premium" or the difference between long-term and short-term interest rates. The premium is usually positive, but it has tended to fall or even "invert" (with the short rate exceeding the long rate) as short rates increase late in a cyclical upswing. Bond market and Fed reactions that provoke the inversion have been triggered by a rising wage share along with other factors.

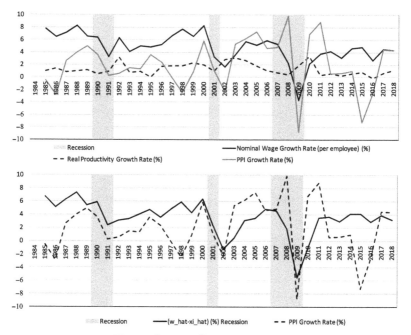

FIGURE I.2 Wage and price inflation rates

world complications such as the drop in producer prices in 2015 that was due to collapsing energy costs). Peak growth rates of labor cost have gone down by more than 3 percentage points since the 1980s, pulling down price inflation. In turn, interest rates have declined, driving up capital gains in conjunction with rising profits (details in Chapter 3).

POLITICAL ECONOMY

It is helpful to look at these results against a political economy background. Two classics are relevant. One is Karl Polanyi's book on *The Great Transformation* (1944). W. Arthur Lewis (1954) on economic development provides a natural extension to economic duality as reflected in the structure of production. The American economy has been running the processes Polanyi and Lewis describe in reverse. For example, the macroeconomic capital/output ratio has fallen and the profit share of output has gone up, contrary to the standard macro-economic scenario. Reversing Lewis's narrative about economic development, employment and the structure of production have shifted toward sectors with low growth and levels of real wages and productivity. All these trends benefit households at the tip of the income distribution.

Polanyi's analysis is historically sophisticated and profound – we can only scratch the surface here. He discussed economic change beginning in the eighteenth century in terms of "fictitious commod-ities" including labor, land, and money (linked to world economic relations). For most economists these "commodities" are the usual macro variables, but Polanyi concentrated on how they are "embedded" in the socioeconomic system. The US economy is now splitting into separate dual zones in all three dimensions. At the macro level, distributions of labor income, land rents, and financial flows have become more unequal, reflecting the devolution of market power from labor to capital.

Polanyi also saw a dialectical process in the flourishing of what is now called free market economics or laissez-faire in the nineteenth century, which he said was "planned." Then a political response led to a "double movement" reasserting social concerns. The dialectic con-tinued into the twentieth century with the rise and fall of Fascism. Growing incomes in the nineteenth century were almost destroyed by the upheavals of the twentieth. Now in the twenty-first century, the tide of laissez-faire is again in flood. In response to political forces, will it eventually ebb and fall in a new double movement? If it does, the relevant time frame must be measured in decades, not just years.

OTHER PERSPECTIVES

There are of course many other ways of analyzing distributional change. Detailed microeconomic factors are summarized in Chapter 5.

Regulatory and institutional factors helped hold wage increases below growth of productivity. They include austerity, both as a macroeconomic practice and as an ideology supporting anti-labor interventions. Political conflict has been the linchpin of increasingly hostile National Labor Relations Board policies toward unions. Many states have their own right-to-work laws. Also entering are divide-and-rule employer tactics in "fissuring" labor markets, nonpoaching and noncompetition clauses in contracts, stagnant minimum wages (now sporadically increasing), and a low ratio of employment to population (now also rising). Changes in trade and technology have reduced labor's bargaining power (e.g., globalization and outsourcing). So have robots (the latest media fad). They are mostly important in the automobile industry, boosting inequality across states and regions. Perhaps 5–10 percent of jobs are at high risk from automation.

In product markets, profits have been supported by less aggressive antitrust intervention. Chicago economics led to an exclusive focus on price competition and the ideology of shareholder value maximization. Product market concentration has risen, and there are specific industry trends such as the emergence of platform companies. But information and relevant parts of retail sectors are less than 10 percent of GDP.

No matter how detailed, micro studies beg the question of how their findings generalize to the macro or sectoral level; for example, "superstar" firms are another recent fad. They occupy the "fat tail" of an earnings distribution typically skewed to the right. Their high productivity may drive down the average sectoral wage share. But then what are the institutional barriers that prevent workers in these firms from getting higher pay? We are back to wage repression. Recent studies suggest that there is substantial churn among superstar firms and sectors. They do not have "super" sustained productivity growth.

Rents are another mainstream trope. Since Ricardo, they are understood as deriving from demand for a service or asset controlled by some economic actor. But then, what is the source of demand? Will it grow faster than productivity, raising the profit share? Operating in the property market, the "real estate rental and leasing" sector generates more than 25 percent of total profits. Its own-profit share of value-added is very high, over 90 percent. But its own-profit and value-added shares have increased slowly. The sector is not a big source of *rising* profit inequality.

On another front, highly paid executives are also said to receive their high incomes due to "rents." What is the source of demand? What is the institutional basis? Why is there increasing social acceptance of extremely high pay? Rules of the game and institutions matter. Certainly there is more US tolerance for outrageous pay now than in the past, but that can change, as it has before; for example, during the New Deal.

It remains to be seen if a double movement along Polanyi's lines can turn around adverse distributional trends as in the simulation results. It is difficult to imagine that democracy can be compatible with another fifty years of rising inequality.

I   Decades of Income Inequality

Economic inequality in the United States began an upward march around 1970. As of 2019, the pace may have slowed but any changes were far from reversing almost five decades of distributional deterioration.

Inequality's ascent can be tracked from two angles – income and wealth. This chapter will look at rising income disparity across households. Chapter 2 shows how income differences showed up macroeconomically. Chapter 3 addresses the distribution of wealth at the macroeconomic and household levels, and Chapter 4 examines the sectoral structure of production.

Income and wealth distributions are multidimensional, but American experience can be understood in terms of a three-way breakdown of households: the rich, represented by the top 1 percent in the size distribution of income, the middle class, and a large group more or less below the midline. The classes differ both in sources of income and the ways that they use it.

The top 1 percent comprises about 1.2 million households with incomes of a few hundred thousand up through millions of dollars per year. The Congressional Budget Office (CBO) data underlying this study direct attention toward this richest 1 percent in the size distribution of income.

The group just below is the "middle class." There is no hard-and-fast definition. Using the data organized by the groups in Figure 1.1, it is convenient to focus on 47 million households between the 61st and 99th percentiles of the income distribution. Their average (or mean) income is around $160,000, mostly from labor compensation as opposed to the top 1 percent's earnings from capital and other sources. They have positive saving and visible wealth.

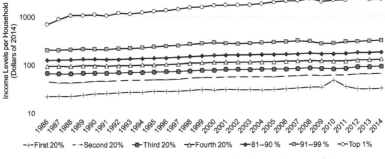

FIGURE 1.1 Income levels per household (logarithmic scale)

At the bottom are households between the 1st and 60th percentiles. A significant fraction of their income comes from public transfer programs. The data suggest that households falling in this group spend more money than they receive and so have negative saving. Consistent with this observation, they have accumulated negligible net worth or wealth.

As discussed in more detail in Chapter 2, in 2014, the top group received around 18 percent of household income, not including capital gains, of which they received a disproportionate share. Households between the 61st and 99th percentiles took in 53 percent, and the bottom three-fifths shared the remaining 29 percent. The share of the top 1 percent doubled over three decades after the mid-1980s.

THE DATA

Sorting households by income groups follows the common practice of describing the size distribution in terms of quantiles defined by shares of the total – the top 1 percent, the bottom 60 percent, etc. Over time, some households will of course cross the income-level boundaries separating the groups but such micro-level detail is ignored in this and many other studies.

The *income* of a household sums up its flows of receipts coming from various sources, which differ across the size distribution. A *household* is a stable collection of people living under the same roof (or, for the well-off, roofs). A useful reference frame is *gross domestic product* or GDP. The interpretation here is that the cost, including imports, of supplying goods and services is equal to the value of the economy's aggregate demand, which comprises (i) household and government consumption, (ii) capital formation (investment, in economist speak) by households, business, and government, and (iii) exports.

With a bit of fudging, components of supply and demand are estimated by official agencies (the Bureau of Economic Analysis or BEA in the United States) on the basis of market transactions. The independently calculated totals of output (demand) and income (cost) typically lie within a percent or less of one another (the so-called "statistical discrepancy" is small). The national income and product accounts (NIPA) quantify GDP, itself defined as total demand (= total cost) minus imports.

NIPA data are extended in this book to include distribution. In the USA, as opposed to many developing countries, not much work has been done on linking survey-based information on key distributive variables (types of income and expenditure including transfers received, taxes paid, consumption, saving) for swaths of the size distribution to the national accounts. Our major sources of data were studies by the CBO and the Consumer Expenditure Survey (CEX) of the Bureau of Labor Statistics (BLS). The appendix to Chapter 2 describes how we rescaled their estimates to create a representation of the size distribution consistent with the NIPA. The numbers provide a broad-brush representation of the distributive situation for the period 1986–2013, extrapolated to 2014. They are broadly consistent with other studies.

Wealth or *net worth* of a household is the value of its assets (real estate, other physical capital, and financial holdings) minus its liabilities. Wealth can rise over time due to saving from current income and capital gains due to rising prices of existing assets such as corporate shares and real estate. The details are covered in Chapters 2 and 3, but for the moment we can observe that households with high net worth have the upper hand because they already have high incomes and high saving rates. Since the 1970s they have had access to dividends, interest, and capital gains generated by rising profits. They have also taken in growing labor payments including nonwage incomes such as bonuses and options. All these receipts have supported accumulation of wealth.

Such fair fortune has not always been the case. The share in wealth of rich households was around 50 percent just prior to the Great Depression, fell to 25 percent in the 1960s, and is now in the vicinity of 40 percent. By around 1980, high New Deal taxes had been defanged and a stagnant stock market began a long upswing. Along with higher distributed profits these developments generated pleasantly rising net worth at the top while the rest of the population got left behind.

INEQUALITY IN INCOME

The task at hand is to present details about sources of incomes and how they were used. Economy-wide, the biggest flow of income is labor compensation, including wages and supplements such as employers' contributions to social security, insurance, pension funds, etc. Principally to the benefit of the top 1 percent, compensation also includes profit-related payments such as bonuses and stock options.

Total compensation of all groups is around 60 percent of household income in the NIPA. Besides employees' pay, other incomes such as proprietors' receipts, rent, and depreciation on real estate figure into the cost of producing GDP, and amount to 12 percent of the household total. The remaining 28 percent of income takes the form of transfers from other economic entities: nonfinancial and financial business, the government, and the rest of the world. Government transfers make up 16 percent and interest and dividends generated by domestic and foreign business profits amount to 12 percent.

Finally, capital gains due to price increases of real estate and corporate equity are "real money" for households but are *not* included in GDP because they do not figure into the cost of production. Household capital gains fluctuate from year to year. According to the CBO data, recently that have ranged from 1 percent (in 2008) to more than 5 percent (2013) of GDP. On a per household basis, 70 percent of income from capital gains flows toward the top 1 percent.

TRENDS IN INCOME DISTRIBUTION

Over the recent period, all payments except government transfers have become more concentrated. Modest expansion of the welfare state has not been able to offset increasing inequality of the other income flows. As shown in Chapter 2, including capital gains, the top 1 percent enjoyed an 8 percentage-point boost in their income share. Supported by transfers, the share of overall income of the bottom 60 percent decreased slightly, so that the middle class got the squeeze.

Figure 1.1 provides an overall picture of trends in distribution across the CBO's seven income groups, the biggest takeaway being the vast spread between incomes of the top 1 percent and the rest. To get all the groups into one diagram, incomes per household are plotted with a logarithmic scale on the vertical axis. Even with the scale adjustment, the income advantage of the rich stands out. Moreover, it increased steadily over time.

To provide perspective, a lucky wage earner in the bottom 20 percent might receive $10 per hour. His or her household might earn not much more than $20,000 per year. A household in the top 1 percent might bring in $2 million over the same time period. Figure 1.1 suggests that this hundredfold difference is more than twice its level in the mid-1980s.

Seven groups are a lot to keep track of. As noted above, shifts among three income groups – the bottom 60 percent, middle 39 percent, and top 1 percent – illustrate the main trends in inequality, based on data on their mean annual incomes and expenditures per household.

PALMA RATIOS AND INCOME DISTRIBUTION
ACROSS THE THREE GROUPS

As noted in the Introduction, one way to depict inequality is with "Palma (2009) ratios" of the mean incomes of the top 1 percent to incomes of the lower two groups. The ratios highlight the discrepancy between the top group and the rest of the population. Figure 1.2 shows how they rose for both total and disposable incomes per household. The very high ratios at the end of the period did not materialize overnight. It took decades of unequal economic growth to make them exist. The growth rates of the Palmas were in the range of 3 percent per year – an astonishingly high number for *any* macroeconomic ratio over such a long period.

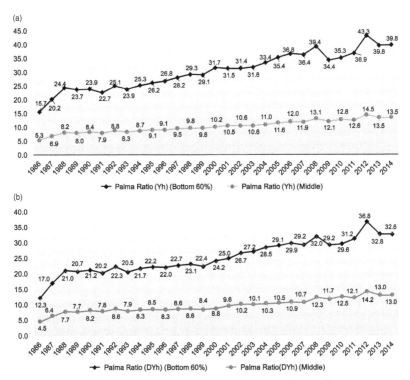

FIGURE 1.2 Palma ratios for top 1 percent vs. 61st to 99th percentile households and lower 60 percent (a) Based on total income per household (Yh) (b) Based on disposable income per household (DYh)

LAGGING REAL WAGES

Let's look at the numbers in a bit more detail, beginning with labor compensation including the supplements mentioned above as the major source. The broad picture of wage growth versus productivity growth has already been presented in Figure I.1. It shows up again in Figure 1.3 in the recent histories of real GDP and real labor income per household.

As noted in the Introduction, "productivity," or the ratio of output to employment, plays a dual accounting role for economic growth because it describes both employment and distribution. Productivity growth is often credited to "technological progress" due to reorganization of production, more efficient capital goods, or better use of capital. In practice, it may arise from greater labor exploitation including wage suppression or sharper competitive practices on the part of business. Regardless of whatever forces it embodies, productivity enters the discussion throughout this book.

The message of Figure 1.3 is that real labor payments did not rise as rapidly as productivity (the scaling in the diagram by the number of households as opposed to person-hours employed does not alter this conclusion). "Technology" per se is not an adequate explanation for the phenomenon. Rather, social forces and policy changes directed

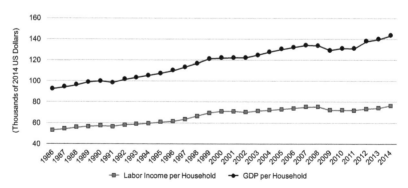

FIGURE I.3 Real GDP and real labor compensation per household over time

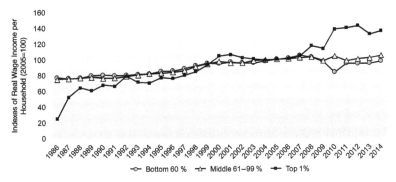

FIGURE 1.4 Indexes of labor compensation

income flows away from wages and toward profits, with highly unequalizing distributive consequences, mostly in favor of high-income earners.

The less-rapid growth of labor payments is striking – roughly 1.7 percent per year as opposed to 2.1 percent for output. The implication is that distribution shifted strongly in favor of nonwage incomes (their ratio to GDP rose by 12 percent over thirty years, in line with the growth of the profit share). Most of the small overall wage increases in Figure 1.3 went to the top 1 percent.

Side-stepping the log scale in Figure 1.1, Figure 1.4 shows indexes of labor compensation per household centered on a level of 100 in 2005. The rapid growth for the top group stands out. Compensation growth for the other two groups was far more modest.

HIGH-INCOME HOUSEHOLDS

This shift to nonwage income is striking for households in the top 1 percent. These people generate most personal saving and hold substantial wealth, including equity and real estate, which produce capital gains. Figure 1.5 shows how their average (mean) income along with its sources went up over time – late in the period rich households received more than $2 million per year. Note that the CBO distributional data only allow analysis of *mean* ("average") incomes by group.

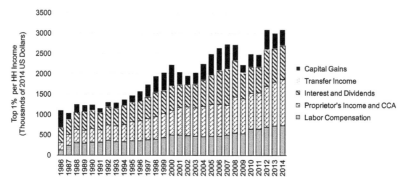

FIGURE 1.5 Real per household incomes, top 1 percent

Especially for the top 1 percent, the mean will exceed the *median* because the distribution within this group is skewed to the right or has a "fat tail" (including billionaires at the far end of the curve). This applies to all observations about mean incomes in this book, more strongly for the top group than the bottom.

The bottom segments of the bars show that rich households received substantial labor compensation. As already noted, it includes much income from bonuses and stock options, which look more like payments to capital than labor. "Workers" such as executives at the top of large nonfinancial and financial corporations drive up the earnings numbers.

The average amounts are indeed large, ranging upwards of $500,000 per year at the end of the period. They more than doubled over a generation. On the other hand, rich households take in only about 7 percent of total labor income (4 percent of GDP) economy-wide. Most of their money comes from other sources. Figure 1.5 shows that "proprietors' incomes," along with rents and depreciation (capital consumption allowances or CCA, included for consistency with the double entry bookkeeping of the national accounts), exceeded labor income. Depending on the year in question, interest and dividends tended to be the same as or larger than earnings from employment. Capital gains on equity and real estate usually ranged in the hundreds of thousands per household per year. Nonwage income per wealthy household roughly doubled between 1986 and 2014, for a growth rate close to 3 percent per year, much faster than the growth of output.

A final striking feature of Figure 1.5 is that, apart from the miniscule transfers, *all* forms of income received by rich households grew steadily over time. The steep slopes of the Palma ratios in Figure 1.2 were supported by diverse payments, which increased reliably. Reversing such trends will not be easy.

Total pretax income of the upper 1 percent in 2014 was $2.7 trillion. GDP was $17.4 trillion; so, that group took in 15.7 percent of output. Including capital gains, they got close to $3 trillion. More than 15 percent of GDP in the hands of a small proportion of households represents enormous economic power.

It is not quite accurate to call the top 1 percent "capitalists" or "rentiers" in the traditional senses of the words, but they are not far removed. Their rapid income growth mostly came from financial transfers and management, not from work on production or direct provision of useful services.

MIDDLE CLASS AND LOW-INCOME HOUSEHOLDS

Members of the middle class look more like "workers." Figure 1.6 shows their income sources. In line with Figure 1.1, note the difference in the vertical axis scales between Figures 1.5 (zero to 3,500 in thousands of 2014 US dollars) and 1.6 (zero to 200 in thousands of 2014 US dollars). The top 1 percent's income is a factor of ten higher than the middle class's. It simply does not fit with flows to the other 99 percent of households.

The bars show that labor compensation makes up almost 70 percent of middle incomes. In the US, around 7 percent of total compensation is immediately removed by taxes for Social Security and Medicare (flowing via FICA, Federal Insurance and Contributions) so the numbers are less rosy than they look.

The real mean pretax compensation average for middle-class households increased from around $95,000 in 1986 to $130,000 in 2014 – a modest growth rate of 1 percent per year. Other significant,

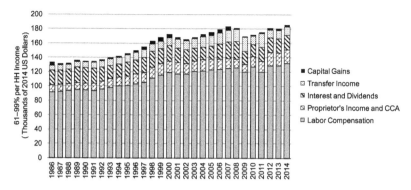

FIGURE 1.6 Real per household incomes, 61–99 percent

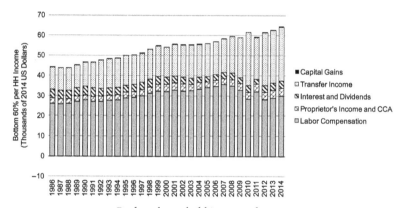

FIGURE 1.7 Real per household incomes, bottom 60 percent

though secondary, middle-class income sources are interest and dividends, and proprietors' incomes. There are also government transfers. The main components are medical (Medicare, Medicaid, and other) at about 6 percent of GDP and Social Security (pensions and disability) at about 5 percent. Almost sixty other programs add up to another 3 percent. Total transfers exceed FICA taxes. As will be seen, the net income flow benefits the bottom 60 percent, not the middle class.

Households in the bottom 60 percent of the income distribution are far more dependent on transfers, as shown in Figure 1.7. Even with $25,000 of transfer support coming in, relatively poor households had a mean income of $55,000 or one-third of the middle-class level (as reflected in the different vertical scales of Figures 1.6 and 1.7). Annual wage income per household is around $30,000. Average hours worked per year in the USA is around 1,800, so employed people in a household with two full-time earners were getting about $8.30 per hour before paying social contributions. (The corresponding figure for the middle class is $30.40.) They received only a few thousand dollars in the form of financial, rental, and proprietors' incomes.

COMPLICATIONS WITH SAVING

Households use their incomes for various purposes. Five are considered here: consumption, direct taxes, contributions to social insurance (the FICA tax), interest paid, and saving. The big mystery involves saving, usually estimated as a residual in consumer expenditure surveys and the national accounts. Saving is a small number in comparison to directly observed uses of income such as consumption and taxes; so, the imprecision in its reported level is high.

Fuzzy numbers about saving rates from income are unfortunate, since they enter into determination of effective demand. As will be seen, saving plus capital gains determines accumulation of wealth. It is also worth noting that household saving is only about one quarter of the total for the private sector (households and corporations). As discussed in Chapter 2 and Taylor (2017), the action in private saving is provided by business.

Further complications arise. One, emphasized by Carvalho and Rezai (2016), is that expenditure-survey saving rates for the lower classes are consistently negative. An OECD study (Fesseau and van de Ven, 2014) reports negative rates for the bottom three or four quintiles of the household income distribution for eight countries including the USA. The usual explanations include "under the table" wage payments in the form of cash and unremunerated services, informal transfers among family and other groups, unpaid debt, and movements of households across boundaries of income bins. The first factors mentioned would be part of the hidden or shadow economy based upon payments flows not captured in official statistics. It is typically estimated to be in the range of 8–10 percent of GDP in the USA.

Moreover, overall saving estimates from consumer budget surveys and the national accounts are not consistent (i.e., summing saving of all households in the BLS CEX survey and extrapolating to the macro level produces a number different from the estimate of saving in the NIPA). We finessed this problem by *assuming* saving rates were equal to –0.182 for the bottom group of households and 0.405 for the top (broadly consistent with the CEX), applying them to total incomes summarized above, and then adjusting the middle-class rate to set annual total saving equal to the NIPA total. That rate varied between 0.05 and 0.17 in the calculations over the years, in the range that can be derived from the CEX. Dissaving by the bottom 60 percent was around 5 percent of GDP, presumably in the shadow economy.

Finally, besides being a residual in the data, saving is an afterthought in sensible demand-driven macro modeling. Households receive incomes and pay taxes, consume, etc. from them. Saving is what is left over, but in models that follow Keynes, the key behavioral relationship is consumption as a function of income. It is often convenient to express household consumption in terms of saving and tax parameters, but that is only a mathematical shortcut – effective demand drives the system.

USES OF INCOMES

Figure 1.8 summarizes use of income by the top 1 percent. In the overall picture, their interest payments and social contributions are minimal. (The 2018 social security tax cap for an individual was $7,961, trifling in comparison to household incomes in the millions.) The major outflows are for consumption, saving, and direct taxes (the latter at a rate of 22 percent of income in 2014). The key observation is that high-income recipients save close to half the money they take in – a major contribution to growing wealth inequality per household.

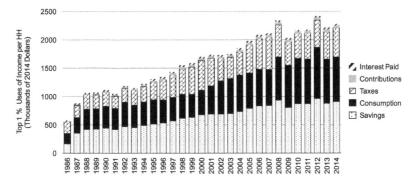

FIGURE 1.8 Uses of real per household incomes, top 1 percent

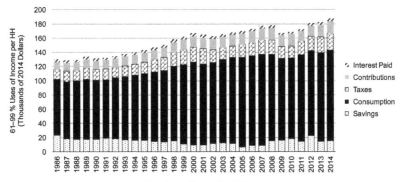

FIGURE 1.9 Uses of real per household incomes, 61–99 percent

The picture in Figure 1.9 for the middle class is rather different. The dominant entry is for consumption, with visible outlays for saving, direct taxes, and social contributions. These households receive 55 percent of income, so in 2014, as a group, they saved $700 billion as compared to $1.1 trillion for the top 1 percent (of course saving per household is far higher at the top). Their total tax rate, including direct taxes *and* FICA contributions, is 22 percent, just like the richer households. Social contributions fluctuated in the range of transfers received so the middle class had, at most, modest benefits from the welfare state.

The negative saving of the bottom 60 percent of households shows up in the bars below the horizontal axis in Figure 1.10. Their

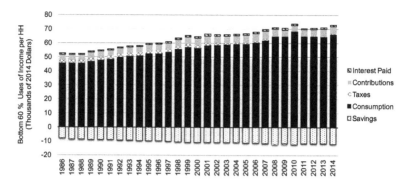

FIGURE I.10 Uses of real per household incomes, bottom 60 percent

consumption, along with an 8 percent outlay for social contributions, exceeds income. Interest paid and direct taxes are unimportant.

SOCIAL VS. MARKET FORCES

In the next chapter we will see how the three groups of households, along with business, government, and the rest of the world, fit into the overall macroeconomy. The main point that emerges from this first look at the data is that the USA truly has a three-class economy. There is a rich, self-perpetuating quasi-capitalist group at the top that relies principally on profit-related incomes, a middle class with most of its income coming from wages, and 60 percent of the population living on a combination of relatively low wages and transfers.

Over decades, several cumulative distributive trends stand out.

As already noted, labor compensation lagged the growth of output; in the jargon, real wages grew less rapidly than labor productivity. The wage share of income fell, and the profit share went up.

Labor payments at the very top grew much more rapidly than the average economywide. They roughly tripled over twenty-five years, a growth rate of 4.5 percent per year.

Even so, the bulk of income of the top 1 percent came from nonwage sources.

Labor is the main income source for the middle class, whose average per household income grew only half a percent per year. The poorest 60 percent fared no better, although their transfer incomes did trend upward.

Rich households had high incomes (including capital gains) and high saving rates. Palma ratios of incomes per household for the top versus the lower groups grew steadily at high rates. Unsurprisingly, the share of the top 1 percent in total wealth went up rapidly, as will be discussed further in Chapter 3.

2 Macroeconomic Income Distribution

"What news on the Rialto?" For the financial players of the *Merchant of Venice*, the shipping news was about gains and losses in the accounts of the parties concerned (pounds of flesh excluded). Double-entry bookkeeping to track market transactions was standard Venetian practice long before Shakespeare had Salanio and Salarino discussing nautical finance in Act One. Centuries later, double entries were extended to national income by John Maynard Keynes (1940) in his pamphlet on *How to Pay for the War*.

Here we show how the distributive data from Chapter 1 can be folded into the NIPA system patterned after his work, first for a single household and then for all three. A natural extension to wealth accounting via "flows of funds" is then taken up.

SOCIAL ACCOUNTING MATRICES
AND NATIONAL ACCOUNTS

Double-entry accounting fits naturally into a spreadsheet or matrix formulation as Keynes's student Richard Stone (1966) pointed out. He coined the label "social accounting matrix" or SAM for a representation of the national accounts. A US version for 2014 appears in Figure 2.1. The official NIPA accounts could be expressed in matrix form, but the BEA chooses not to pursue that route. The appendix to this chapter sketches how we extended the matrix in Figure 2.1 to incorporate income inequality.

It makes sense to walk through the payment flows in the spreadsheet to see how they interact with distribution. Figure 2.1, set up in units of trillions of dollars per year, provides an introduction. It is built around an aggregated single household sector (we'll get to the three classes a bit later), business, government at all levels, and the rest of

2014 SAM – Macro Level (Trillions of Dollars)

2014			CURRENT EXPENDITURE					CAPITAL EXPENDITURE			TOTAL	GDP
			Households	BUS	GOV	ROW	INT & DIV	HOU	BUS	GOV		
HOU	Uses of Total Supply	11.66	11.87		2.56	2.34		0.60	2.26	0.60	20.22	17.35
	Labor Wages	7.89		0.04	2.49		1.96				16.15	
	Labor Contributions	1.36										
	Non Labor Income — Prop.inc., rents, etc. 1.96 / CCA 0.45	2.41										
BUS	Profits — Net Profits 2.26 / CCA 1.78	4.04				0.39	2.27				6.69	
	Transfers											
	Int Div											
GOV	Indirect Taxes, CCA and OS — Indirect Taxes etc. 1.14 / CCA 0.52	1.65	3.04	0.61		0.02	0.13				5.45	
	Direct Taxes	1.78										
	Contributions Received	1.26										
	Int Div											
ROW	Imports	2.87	0.06	0.15	0.07		0.47				3.62	
	Transfers											
	Int Div											
INT DIV Disbursed			0.26	3.48	0.62	0.47					4.83	
Total Expenditures		20.22	15.23	4.28	5.74	3.22	4.83	0.60	2.26	0.60	36.75	

NET LENDING

	Households	BUS	GOV	ROW	INT & DIV	HOU	BUS	GOV	TOTAL
HOU	0.92					-0.60			*0.32*
BUS		2.42					-2.26		*0.32*
GOV			-0.29					-0.60	*-0.88*
ROW				0.41					*0.41*
INT DIV					0.00				*0.00*
BALANCE									*0.00*

FIGURE 2.1 Macro level SAM for 2014

the world. There is also a "financial" sector, which collects interest and dividends from the four others and then redistributes all these payments. This accounting trick avoids the need to present bilateral financial transfers among the sectors. The BEA accounts also include several transfer flows that do not go through finance. They are "small," tens or hundreds of billions of dollars per year, relative to $17.35 trillion of GDP or about 0.1 percent of the total. With two digits displayed after the decimal point, these minor entries clutter Figure 2.1 but are largely ignored in the following discussion.

DEMAND AND COSTS

The SAM is set up around several accounting conventions. One is that sums of the entries in corresponding rows and columns should be equal. For example, total demand of 20.22 (trillion dollars) in the first row equals overall cost of supply (including imports of 2.87) in the first column.[1] Total household income of 16.15 in the second row equals the sum of entries for expenditures (15.23) and saving (0.92) in the corresponding column.

The first row sets out the composition of demand. "Current" expenditures include consumption of goods and services by households and government (11.87 and 2.56 respectively) and exports to the rest of the world (2.34). There is also "capital spending" by households, business, and government including increases in inventories and gross fixed capital formation, which economists as opposed to financial players call "investment." For simplicity, we consolidate inventory changes with capital formation. In practice, investment is further divided into net investment and depreciation (or CCA).[2] CCA is omitted along the row to save space.

Costs of supply are listed down the first column. The big items are payments to labor including "contributions" (11.66) and business

---

[1]   To save space, the word "trillion" is omitted from the description of many flows in the SAM. It is mentioned where it matters.

[2]   In national accounts nomenclature, depreciation is called capital consumption allowance, or CCA.

profits (4.04). Households also receive nonlabor income (2.41). CCA of 0.45 is one component. Because it is included in demand, by double-entry principles CCA by sector must also enter into costs. Total investment by households in row one is 0.6. Subtracting CCA gives household net investment or new capital formation of 0.15. The remaining household nonlabor income includes proprietors' revenue (around 70 percent of the total of 1.96) and "rents on owner-occupied housing."[3]

Business gets gross profits of 4.04. Subtracting CCA of 1.78 sets net profits equal to 2.26. From the first row, business net investment is 2.26 − 1.78 = 0.48. With profits exceeding investment, business has room to pay direct taxes and transfer profit income via the financial sector to, mainly, households. Government's contribution to cost comes from indirect taxes and CCA. GDP equals total output minus imports. Its level is 17.35.

INCOMES, TRANSFERS, AND SPENDING

Chapter 1 shows that transfer payments – governmental for the poor and middle class, financial for the middle class and rich – play key roles in the household income distribution. The macroeconomic implications need to be traced.

According to SAM accounting, rows below the top one in Figure 2.1 summarize incomes. Columns present expenditures. Outlays including saving (used in practice to pay for investment and purchases minus sales of financial assets) must equal incomes for all sectors. As we have seen, households get money from labor payments and nonlabor incomes as costs of producing goods and services. Transfer flows come from government (2.49) and finance (1.96). As noted above, income is 16.15, so that transfers provide more than one-quarter of the total. Income is disbursed down the relevant column for consumption, direct and employment taxes, financial payments, and (at the bottom of the array) saving.

---

[3] Such "imputed rents" are the cost column's counterpart to households' estimated own-consumption of housing services in the top row of the SAM. They have long been controversial in national income accounting. They should be distinguished from profits in the "real estate rental and leasing" sector discussed in Chapters 4 and 5.

Household direct taxes (1.78) and social contributions including FICA (1.26) add up to 3.04. Government also receives indirect taxes on production, direct taxes on business and the rest of the world, and transfers from finance. Its total income is 5.45, or 31 percent of GDP. This share might be compared to levels approaching 50 percent in countries in Western Europe. Households' incoming transfers of 2.49 exceed their social contributions (1.26), but are less than their total payments to government (3.04). The fiscal transfer flow is 14.5 percent of GDP, which can be compared to 25–30 percent in the prosperous corner of Europe.

The next step is to examine how all these flows are spread across the three household groups. Figure 2.2 gives the breakdown. The bottom 60 percent pay 0.33 into the government (mostly FICA contributions) and get 1.92 back, thereby picking up 1.59 trillion dollars or about 9 percent of GDP. The middle class gets 0.55 in transfers and pays 0.86 in contributions, losing 2 percent of GDP to the welfare state. With direct taxes of 1.01, their total tax is 1.87. The top 1 percent pay 0.06 in contributions and get 0.02 in transfers. Their direct tax burden is 0.7. Direct taxes help finance government investment (0.6) and consumption of goods and services (2.56).

SQUEEZE ON THE MIDDLE CLASS

Mapping the income distribution into three groups raises questions about which gained or lost incomes over time. As Figures 2.3 and 2.4 illustrate, the middle class took the major hit from the income gains of the top 1 percent. In the first diagram for the cost-based "primary" income distribution (shown in the first column of the SAM in Figure 2.2), the combined share of profits and the top 1 percent rose by around 8 percentage points over almost twenty years; the share of the poor income group fell by 2 or 3 points.

There was a clear income squeeze for the middle class. It had to absorb the difference between the 8-point increase at the top and 2-point fall at the bottom. A similar picture appears in Figure 2.4. The top 1 percent receives around 70 percent of capital gains (described more fully

2014 SAM with 3 classes in trillions

2014	Supply	CURRENT EXPENDITURE — HOU Bottom 60th	Mid 61–99%	Top 1%	BUS	GOV	ROW	INT & DIV	CAP. HOU	CAP. BUS	CAP. GOV	TOTAL	GDP
Uses of Total Supply		5.09	5.83	0.95	0.03	2.56	2.34		0.60	2.26	0.60	**20.22**	**17.35**
HOU — Bottom 60th	**2.47**				0.03	1.92		0.24				**4.66**	
Labor Wages	1.85												
Labor Contributions	0.32												
Non Labor Income	0.29				0.03	1.92		0.24					
Mid 61–99th	**7.14**				0.01	0.55		0.88				**8.58**	
Labor Wages	5.28												
Labor Contributions	0.98												
Non Labor Income	0.88				0.01	0.55		0.88					
Top 1%	**2.05**				0.00	0.02		0.84				**2.91**	
Labor Wages	0.76												
Labor contributions	0.05												
Non Labor Income	1.24				0.00	0.02		0.84					
BUS	**4.04**						0.39	2.27				**6.69**	
Profits	4.04												
Transfers						0.02	0.39						
Int Div								2.27					
GOV	**1.65**	0.40	1.88	0.76	0.61		0.02	0.13				**5.45**	
Indirect Taxes, CCA and OS	1.65												
Direct Taxes		0.07	1.01	0.70	0.61								
Contributions Received		0.33	0.86	0.06									
Int Div								0.13					
ROW	**2.87**	0.02	0.04	0.00	0.15	0.07		0.48				**3.62**	
Imports	2.87	0.02	0.04	0.00	0.15	0.07							
Transfers													
Int Div								0.48					
INT DIV Disbursed		**0.08**	**0.15**	**0.03**	**3.48**	**0.62**	**0.47**					**4.83**	
Total Expenditures		**5.59**	**7.89**	**1.75**	**4.28**	**5.74**	**3.22**	**4.83**	**0.60**	**2.26**	**0.60**	**36.75**	

NET LENDING

	Bottom 60th	Mid 61–99%	Top 1%	BUS	GOV	ROW	HOU	BUS	GOV	TOTAL
	−0.93	0.68	1.17	2.42	−0.29	0.41				
HOU — Bottom 60th							0.18			**0.32**
Mid 61–99th							0.34			**0.15**
Top 1%							0.07			**−0.88**
BUS								−2.26		**0.41**
GOV						−0.29		−0.60		**0.00**
ROW				2.42			−0.60			**0.00**
INT DIV						0.41				**0.00**
BALANCE										**0.00**

FIGURE 2.2 SAM for 2014 with three household groups (trillions of dollars)

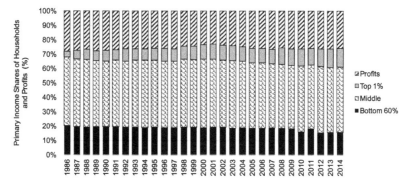

FIGURE 2.3   Shares of profits and households in primary income

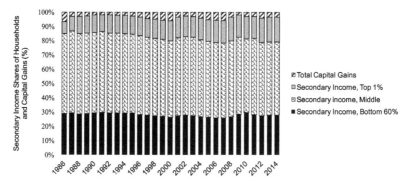

FIGURE 2.4   Household shares of secondary income plus capital gains

in Chapter 3). Thanks to that inflow, its income share went up by 8 points. The share at the bottom fell slightly so again the middle class took the hit.[4] American politics has responded to this relative income shift.

PROFITS, FINANCE, AND WEALTH

To begin to see how profits get channeled to households (especially rich ones) it makes sense to begin with a simplified version of Figure 2.1. Figure 2.5 presents the essentials using symbols, which will prove useful in later discussion. Government, the rest of the world, and

---

[4]   Using "inequality gradients," Kuhn, Schularick, and Steins (2017) map income and wealth changes in more detail, consistently with Figures 2.3 and 2.4.

	Household outlays	Business outlays	Investment	Change in debt	Total
	PC		$PI = PgK =$ $P[(g{-}\delta) + \delta]K$		PX
Household income	wbX		F		Y_h
Net profits CCA	$\pi PX - \delta PK$ δPK				$Y_b =$ $\pi PX = rPK$
Household flows of funds	S_h			$-\dot{D}$	0
Business flows of funds		S_b	$-PI$	$\dot{D}$	0
Total	PX	Y_h	Y_b	0	0

FIGURE 2.5 Rudimentary SAM for households and business (in symbols)

financial details are left out to keep the bookkeeping simple. The double-entry bookkeeping will illustrate how changes in financial transfers and business liabilities (called "debt" in the spreadsheet) balance profits between business and households. Capital gains and losses are brought into the picture in Chapter 3.

Following another SAM accounting convention, all entries in the first row are evaluated at the same price level P (basically the "GDP deflator"). For example, if C^m is the current market value of consumption then its "real" level is defined as $C = C^m/P$, with P being computed as an index number.

Real investment is I, the heart of the economic growth analysis discussed in the following chapters. The real capital stock is K, which in the table is assumed to be valued at P.[5] It is convenient for later use to set $I = gK$. Also, CCA can be set equal to δPK, with δ as a rate of depreciation. Real net (of depreciation) investment becomes $(g - \delta)K$. Using a "dot" to signal the change in capital over time we have $\dot{K} = (g - \delta)K = I - \delta K$. In Chapters 5 and 6, it will be convenient to use a "hat" to indicate a rate of growth, $\hat{K} = \dot{K}/K$ so that $\hat{K} = g - \delta$. Finally, real output is $X = C + I$.

[5]   Estimating K is fraught, but we postpone the details until Chapter 3. Using P instead of a specific capital stock deflator, P_K is a commonly used simplification.

In the first column, let w be the nominal ("money") wage rate as plotted in Figure I.2 and b the labor/output ratio. Nominal labor cost is wbX. Labor productivity is $\xi = 1/b$, and the real wage is $\omega = w/P$. It follows that the share of labor in output is $\psi = \omega/\xi$. As noted in Chapter 1, shifts in productivity help drive movements in output and the income distribution,

If π is the share of profits in output, then (ignoring taxes and subsidies) $\pi + \psi = 1$. Profit income is πPX, received by business. The quantity $\pi PX - \delta PK$ becomes profits net of depreciation. In the relevant row, business income $Y_b = \pi PX$. It can also be written as $Y_b = rPK$ with r as the rate of profit on capital. Evidently, $r = \pi(X/K) = \pi u$ where for future reference we define $u = X/K$ as "capital utilization."

In the column for business outlays, an amount F is transferred to households as interest and dividends (amounting to 1.96 trillion in Figure 2.1) so that their income is $Y_h = wbX + F$. The remaining profits become (gross) business saving $S_b = \pi PX - F$. Household income is used for consumption PC and saving S_h. In the rows for "flows of funds" household and business savings become "sources" of funds which can be used for financial purposes. The convention is that they have positive signs. "Uses" (just business investment in the simplified SAM) carry a negative sign, and sources and uses must sum to zero along each row.

Investment is a key use of funds. It adds PI to demand in the first row and in an accounting trick shows up again as $-PI$ in the business flows of funds. Suppose that business saving falls short of investment so that $S_b < PI$. Then the sector must find another source of funds, say an increase in debt $\dot{D} > 0$. We end up with

$$S_b + \dot{D} - PI = 0. \tag{2.1}$$

For business, the sum of two sources of funds equals one use. Households accept the higher debt as a use of funds so that

$$S_h - \dot{D} = 0. \tag{2.2}$$

These flows are extended in Chapter 3 to include corporate shares.

THE ROLE OF FINANCIAL TRANSFERS

Financial transfers – interest and dividends – have played a key role in raising incomes of the top 1 percent. It makes sense to examine how they fit into the SAM. A "theorem of accounting" stating that $\pi PX = F + S_b$ (profits = financial transfers to households + business saving) follows immediately from the business row and column in Figure 2.5. It is of interest to see how well this observation carries over to the more complicated bookkeeping of Figures 2.1 and 2.2.

In Figure 2.1, households receive 1.96 in interest and dividends and pay 0.26, for a net financial inflow of 1.7. Subtracting from profits gives 4.04 – 1.7 = 2.34. Business saving is 2.42 so the numbers are close. The discrepancy arises because of all the minor transfers. Similar accounting regarding payments from NIPA business profits show up in SAMs for other years.

Figure 2.2 shows that the richest households get a net financial transfer of 0.84 – 0.03 = 0.81, or 48 percent of the total. Much more numerous middle-class households are encumbered by payments on debt. Their net financial inflow comes out as 0.88 – 0.15 = 0.73. Poor households get only 0.16 net.

As discussed in Chapter 3, capital gains are another vehicle for transferring profits to households. If all profits (= 4.04) get shifted via interest, dividends, and capital gains then the *total* financial transfer easily exceeds flows from the government (2.49 from above). In fact, when capital gains are included, financial flows from business to households can be greater than profits. This difference between fiscal and financial transfers is a main reason why growth of income of the 1 percent has been so spectacular in recent decades. Largely driven by taxation, the long downswing in rich households' wealth after 1929, recounted in Chapter 1, shows that regressive redistribution need not rule forever.

Figure 2.6 shows the evidence for the last three decades. Financial transfers to the middle class rose slightly, varying around 800 billion dollars in 2014 (14 thousand per household). Flows to the

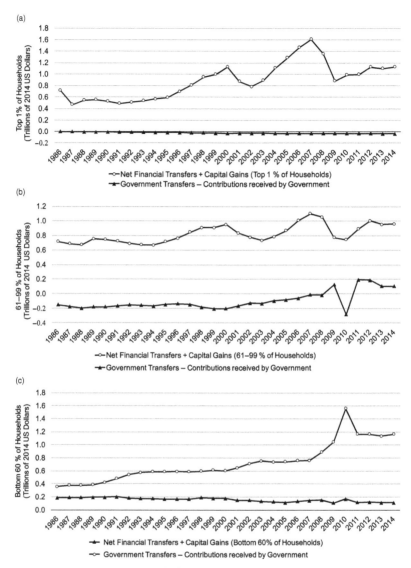

FIGURE 2.6 Household fiscal and financial transfers (a) Top 1 percent (b) Middle class (c) Bottom 60 percent

top 1 percent increased steadily to around 1.2 trillion (over a million per household in good years). Fiscal transfers to the middle class became positive toward the end of the period. The overall fiscal flow went up steadily for the bottom 60 percent, more or less parallel to financial transfers to the rich, but of course spread over 66 million as opposed to 1.2 million households at the end of the period.

ACCOUNTING FOR WEALTH

For future reference, simplified national accounting can be extended to wealth. Figure 2.7 is a wealth accounting matrix or WAM (set up in symbols) based on the Figure 2.5 SAM. The first row shows that household wealth Ω_h is just the total debt claim D against business. Usually in the data, $\Omega_h > 0$. Business holds PK as an asset and has a liability D. Its net worth must be $\Omega_b = PK - D$, which could take either sign. For now we ignore the value of shares issued by business along with the capital gains it – we'll get to them in Chapter 3.

To explore wealth accumulation we can "differentiate balance sheets" to analyze how they change over time. The household row in Figure 2.7 gives $\dot{\Omega}_h = \dot{D}$. Substituting from the flow of funds gives

$$\dot{\Omega}_h = S_h \qquad (2.3)$$

or household wealth accumulation is equal to saving. Similar manipulation shows that business accumulation is

$$\dot{\Omega}_b = S_b - \delta PK \qquad (2.4)$$

so that depreciation of existing capital reduces business wealth.

In Figure 2.1, business net saving is 0.64 = 2.42 – 1.78, giving a modest increase in wealth. Household net saving is 0.47 = 0.92 – 0.45. Figure 2.2 shows, however, that only the two upper household groups

	Capital	Debt	Net worth
Households		D	Ω_h
Business	PK	$-D$	Ω_b
Totals	PK	0	PK

FIGURE 2.7 Rudimentary wealth accounting matrix for households and business (in symbols)

have positive saving. The reported negative saving of poor households implies that they are losing wealth, subject to the reservations mentioned in Chapter 1.[6] All these observations are subject to revision when capital gains and losses are brought into the accounting.

Finally, the last column in Figure 2.7 says that private sector net worth equals the value of the capital stock, $\Omega_h + \Omega_b = PK$. When government and the rest of the world are brought into the accounts, private wealth turns out to be the sum of capital, government debt, and national net foreign assets (negative for the USA).

FLOWS OF FUNDS IN THE DATA

The bookkeeping for flows of funds is more complicated in Figures 2.1 and 2.2 than in Figure 2.5, but the basic set-up is the same. Total household saving is 0.92. The top two groups save 1.17 and 0.68 respectively, offsetting dissaving of –0.93 by poorer households. As a group households invest 0.6. Saving minus investment or "net lending" to the rest of the system is 0.92 – 0.6 = 0.32. In 2014, business saved 2.42 and invested 2.26, so its net lending was 0.15 (after round-off). Depending on the state of the business cycle, business net lending fluctuates between positive and negative over time (Taylor et al. 2008).

Business saving is substantially greater than the flow from households. Ever since Keynes brought up the "propensity to consume" in *The General Theory* (1936) much macroeconomic discussion has centered around household spending and saving.

The truth is that the income that households do *not* spend is much smaller than business profits minus taxes and net financial payments of interest and dividends. In a demand-driven economy, capital accumulation by business is a main driving force, with the sector's retained earnings adjusting accordingly. As discussed further in Chapter 5, Keynes's vision with its emphasis on household saving may have been appropriate for his day, but does not

---

[6]   As discussed in Chapter 6, negative wealth or debt of low income households may dissipate over time, for various reasons.

capture the importance now of government and foreign financial flows. He had to pioneer national income accounting before the significance of military spending, the welfare state, and external trade became clear.

Business saving fluctuates near the sector's level of investment (e.g., 2.26 in Figure 2.1). Similarly, households' saving is usually not far from their own (basically residential) investment of 0.6. Like wages received by the top 1 percent, household saving can be heard but plays second fiddle in the macroeconomic orchestra. There has been a recent resurgence of the "loanable funds" approach to macroeconomics. Because of the evolution in flows of funds as just noted, it makes little sense. The fiscal and foreign accounts play much greater roles than in Keynes's 1930s. For details, see Chapter 5, Taylor (2017), and Storm (2017a).

Government saving is already negative at –0.29. With investment of 0.6, its net borrowing (negative net lending) is 0.89, well above household and business net lending of 0.47. Net lending by all sectors must sum to zero. The rest of the world makes the balance come about. Its "saving," as far as the USA is concerned, is the deficit on current external accounts that must be financed from abroad. The amount in Figure 2.1 is 0.41, which balances the accounts. In 2014, government and foreign deficits were not "twins" since the latter was half-a-trillion dollars greater.

SOCIAL VS. MARKET FORCES

To borrow a phrase from Europe, the US economy is a "transfer union" with two major channels for flows. One involves taxes on labor earnings that help pay for transfers via the welfare state. The other is transformation of profits into interest, dividends, and capital gains via the financial system. In 2014, the financial transfer was around 75 percent bigger than the fiscal.

The magnitude and composition of fiscal transfers are ultimately determined by sociopolitical decisions. Figure 2.6 shows that they increased over time for the bottom 60 percent of house-holds, more or less in line with increasing financial transfers to the top 1 percent. The financial flows – interest, dividends, and capital gains – were nourished by the rising profit share of GDP stemming ultimately from wage repression. Income from capital and the wealth it sustains are the major driving forces for rising inequality in the USA. The open question is whether, in Polanyi's terms, a double movement will redirect these forces.

APPENDIX: NATIONAL ACCOUNTING AND SIZE DISTRIBUTION OF INCOME

For the record, at the cost of a bit of algebra, here is a description of how the data set that integrates the size distribution into the NIPA was put together. It took seven steps.

1. Annual data from the NIPA system were restated as social accounting matrixes (or SAMs). In principle, it should be straightforward to restate national accounts in the form of a SAM, but this step is not normally taken by the Bureau of Economic Analysis. Our methodology was invented several years ago by Nelson Barbosa-Filho (2019).

2. The CBO definitions of income flows for seven household groups were adjusted for rough consistency with the definitions in NIPA (the major arbitrary assumption was to assign one-half each of "other income" flows to financial incomes and wages). This assignment is arbitrary but does align the CBO and NIPA numbers.

3. For each year in the sample, shares of total incomes (including transfers) and taxes for seven household categories were calculated as ratios of flows at the group level to the corresponding totals in the CBO data set.

4. These income shares were then applied to each year's NIPA totals of wages, transfer, financial, and proprietors' incomes to estimate flow levels for the seven income groups. A NIPA-consistent distribution of total income across groups also came out of this calculation. In terms of algebra, let Y_{ij} be the income of household type j from income source i (employment, fiscal transfers, financial transfers, proprietors' and other incomes). Total income of each type from the CBO is Z_i and the total from NIPA is Q_i. We rescaled each household income flow from the CBO to the NIPA according to the

rule $Y_{ij}^* = (Y_{ij}/Z_i)Q_i$. Total rescaled income for household j becomes $Y_j^* = \sum_i (Y_{ij}/Z_i)Q_i$. Because $\sum_j Y_{ij}/Z_i = 1$, it is easy to show that $\sum_j Y_j^* = \sum_i Q_i$. We applied similar rescaling to uses of incomes from CBO data and the Consumer Expenditure Survey (CEX) from the Bureau of Labor Statistics, except that the Y_j^* become control totals for spending levels. Consumption and saving flows were adjusted "by hand" accordingly. The estimates are broadly consistent with the CEX.

5. In more detail, CBO-based shares were used to distribute total NIPA outlays for direct taxes,[7] social insurance, and finance across all seven groups.

6. Shares of total consumption by quintile (adjusted to be consistent with NIPA definitions) from the BLS data were calculated, and then applied to NIPA total consumption. Saving flows by quintile could then be calculated as the differences between income levels and outlays for consumption, finance, and taxes.

7. In Table 2.2, for simplicity, saving rates by income groups were set exogenously and consumption levels followed as residuals. From bottom to top, the postulated saving rates from household incomes were –0.182, 0.091, and 0.405, broadly consistent with BLS numbers.

---

[7] Strictly speaking, the CBO direct tax data refer only to the Federal level while the BEA accounts include state taxes. Our rescaling operation ignored differences in state tax rates, thereby introducing errors in the SAM in the billion dollar range.

3 "Capital," Capital Gains, Capitalization, and Wealth

Capital theory is a small, recondite branch of economics but it can erupt into furious debate about the control of income and wealth. US distributive conflict has brought ancient academic battles to the fore. Capital theory helps shed light on the numbers but it will take some effort to grasp the details.

One way to analyze distribution is in terms of the *size* of households' incomes or holdings of wealth. Alternatively, macroeconomic growth and capital theories analyze the nature or *function* of payments flows, assets, and liabilities. Chapters 1 and 2 provide evidence about how household size distributions of income relate to functional payments flows. The goal of this chapter is to understand linkages between the accumulation of capital and the size distribution of wealth. We start with wealth as treated in macro theories, and then bring in extensions toward size.

CAMBRIDGE CONTROVERSY

In the 1960s, anathemas regarding capital and profits flew between economists at the University of Cambridge in England and opponents at the Massachusetts Institute of Technology in the USA. Along with most American economists, MIT traced the causes of distributional shifts to market forces. The message from Cambridge UK was that economic structure and distribution respond to power relationships and class conflict. Institutional changes furthering wage repression over recent decades are an obvious example. The British won the battle over theory, but lost to massive American forces (including the University of Chicago) in the war about how to teach and practice macroeconomics.[1]

---

[1] When they surface today, results of the controversy are often misstated. For example, the economics commentator John Kay wrote in the *Financial Times* (October 6, 2015)

The Cambridge UK critique showed why mainstream assumptions are not tenable, even if they were to fit the data, which in dynamic terms they do not, as we will see. The gist is that the profit rate r intrinsically enters into the determination of the capital stock K, and so cannot be a well-behaved function thereof. Piero Sraffa (1962), the godfather of the UK Cantabrigians, asked "What is the good of a quantity of capital ... which, since it depends on the rate of interest, cannot be used for its traditional purpose ... to determine the rate of interest [?]"[2]

There are two main branches of capital theory. One, discussed later, values "capital" (in practice a diverse collection of real estate, computer code, and machines) on the basis of the discounted present value of the returns it is supposed to generate. The other focuses on how producers minimize costs of production (including profits) by utilizing labor and capital.

The Cambridge UK vs USA teams took the latter tack, examining least cost "techniques" for combining different sets of capital goods as the rate of profit (r, as defined in Chapter 2) changes. The production cost of each good depends on r along with the prices of the other goods so the interactions are complicated. After the dust had settled, all participants agreed that the same technique could be cheapest to deploy at two or more different levels of r, with other least cost techniques emerging in between. Consequently, there is no clear relationship between the total value of K and r. "Diminishing returns" to capital is not in the cards. The mainstream's

---

that "Robert Solow [from MIT] won easily because of the care he took to specify ... his models" and that the other side was led by the "Cambridge Marxist economist Joan Robinson." In fact, Solow's colleague Paul Samuelson (1966) graciously conceded that MIT was wrong, writing that "We must respect, and appraise, the facts of life." But for ideological reasons, macroeconomics courses at leading US universities did not respect the facts. Twenty years later, MIT's canonical textbook by Olivier Blanchard and Stanley Fischer (1989) did not bother to mention the controversy but was full of neoclassical production theory. Joan Robinson was a left Keynesian, not a Marxist, and a full professor at Cambridge. The classic reference is G. C. Harcourt (1972).

2   Sraffa is using "rate of interest" to refer to what is called the profit rate here.

key assumption about how r and the real wage ω respond to the "size" of the capital stock need not be valid.

CAPITAL AND WEALTH

Because the value of a collection of capital goods can't be nailed down, computing the level of K is inherently fraught. Three procedures, discussed later on, are commonly used to generate a single number to represent capital – perpetual inventory, estimation of the asset price of K from the stock market, and a shortcut called capitalization for computing the discounted present value of the capital collection's returns.

Capital, however estimated, is the main constituent of wealth. Orthodoxy relies on the notion that an economy-wide aggregate K exists, and that it has a close, inverse relationship with r. This linkage is the heart of the standard macroeconomic model of distribution and growth, proposed independently in 1956 by Robert Solow and Trevor Swan. It underlies Piketty's (2014) well-known analysis of increasing concentration of wealth holdings over time.

The assumptions supporting the mainstream relationship are extreme: (i) labor (L) and capital (K) can be measured unambiguously and are fully employed;[3] (ii) output $(X,$ e.g., "real" GDP) is determined from the supply side by an "aggregate production function" based on L and K; (iii) both inputs are subject to decreasing returns to scale in production; (iv) there is a unique saving rate from all income flows to a consolidated private business/household sector (even the rudimentary household class distinctions described in Chapters 1 and 2 are ignored); (v) growth of K is determined by saving; and (vi) growth of the labor supply and employment is set by exogenous population dynamics.

---

[3]   In his *General Theory*, Keynes (1936) dismissively labeled the full employment assertion Say's Law after an early nineteenth century French scholar. The Law implies that any excess of income over consumption and taxes somehow gets automatically translated into an increase in the capital stock. For example, savings newly deposited in a bank immediately get lent to a firm to purchase new equipment or to a contractor to build a house.

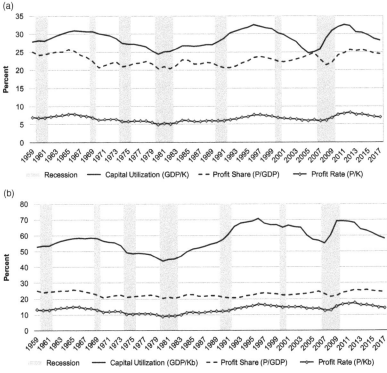

FIGURE 3.1 US output/capital ratio, profit share, and profit rate (a) Based on total capital stock (b) Based on business capital Stock

Assumptions (i) through (iii) set up a "short run" or "temporary equilibrium" describing the economy at a point in time. Then (iv) through (vi) describe how it evolves over time. Chapters 5 and 6 provide more realistic alternative formulations.

In the Solow-Swan model, the fruits of sustained capital accumulation assure that the profit rate will be low, the real wage high, and the income distribution egalitarian in the "long run." We have already seen that, at least for distribution, this scenario has not applied for some time. The evidence is summarized for the national accounts in Figure 3.1. In line with the algebra presented in Chapter 2, $r = \pi u$, with π as the profit share of output and $u = X/K$ as the output/capital ratio. "Capital" K is estimated by the perpetual inventory method, as we will discuss.

The charts show that across US business cycles, the output/ capital ratio u and profit rate r have drifted upward since around 1980. The u ratio based on NIPA business profits moves upward with either total or corporate capital in the denominator. The r ratio for corporate profits rises as well. The profit share goes up and the real wage has been stable.

This history is consistent with the Solow-Swan model *running in reverse*. The economy appears to have "too much" capital per worker. In the world of the model, the K/X and K/L ratios would gradually run down as the system converges toward a "natural" growth rate allegedly set by expansion of the labor force and productivity growth. Given the state of infrastructure and persistent underemployment in the USA, this interpretation looks absurd. With some help from Karl Marx, a more plausible interpretation of recent trends is presented in Chapter 5, which also takes up contemporary mainstream growth theory (which is even weirder than Solow-Swan). Chapter 4 shows how employment and productivity trends across producing sectors also demonstrate retrograde motion.

PERPETUAL INVENTORY

National income statisticians follow most practitioners in falling back on the *perpetual inventory* method to estimate K. It does not take Cambridge complications into account, but at least it does cumulate observed costs of producing new capital goods and how rapidly they depreciate in use. In standard accounting, capital computed in this fashion equals total net worth of the private sector (households with wealth Ω_h and business with Ω_b) emerging from Figure 2.5,

$$\Omega_h + \Omega_b = PK . \tag{3.1}$$

Because $\dot{K} = I - \delta K$, this formula is consistent with the NIPA system which estimates real investment I on the basis of production costs of specific capital goods.

BRINGING IN EQUITY

To simplify the analysis, our initial wealth accounting matrix in Figure 2.5 did not incorporate corporate equity, which underlies the household capital gains discussed in previous chapters. Figure 3.2 sets out balance sheet accounts including equity. According to the accounting conventions built into calculations of national income and flows of funds, both equity and debt are treated as assets of households (positive) and liabilities of firms (negative). To see the details, let E be an index of the volume of corporate shares outstanding, and P_e the equity price. Double-entry bookkeeping requires that the value of equity $P_e E$ enters as a liability of business to balance its placement as an asset of households.

Subject to the adding-up condition (3.1), household wealth is made up of equity and debt issued by business,

$$\Omega_h = P_e E + D. \tag{3.2}$$

Business wealth, meanwhile, is

$$\Omega_b = PK - P_e E - D. \tag{3.3}$$

in other words, the value of capital minus outstanding equity and debt.

These wealth balances result from summing flows of funds over time. It is easy to build equity into a simple SAM as shown in Figure 2.3. You just add a column for "change in equity" with entries of $-P_e \dot{E}$ and $P_e \dot{E}$ in the household and business flow of funds respectively. Then equation (2.2) for household savings is expanded to become

	Capital	Equity	Debt	Net worth
Households		$P_e E$	D	Ω_h
Business	PK	$-P_e E$	$-D$	Ω_b
Totals	PK	0	0	PK

FIGURE 3.2 Rudimentary wealth accounting with capital from perpetual inventory (in symbols)

$$S_h - P_e\dot{E} - \dot{D} = 0. \tag{3.4}$$

In words, household saving is used to buy newly issued equity $\dot{E}$ at the current price P_e and to acquire new debt $\dot{D}$. Extending (2.1), the business flow of funds says that saving plus new issues of equity and debt pay for investment,

$$S_b + \dot{D} + P_e\dot{E} - PI = 0. \tag{3.5}$$

In longstanding US practice, share buybacks (around a trillion dollars in 2018) mean that $\dot{E} < 0$. These share (re)purchases by business transfer money to households. On the other side of the ledger, firms must raise the wherewithal, usually by issuing new debt $\dot{D}$ and/or curtailing investment.[4] In other words, buybacks are a portfolio shift between households, who receive cash in return for giving up shares, and business. If households take up (most of) new business debt, the transaction for them amounts to a debt-for-equity swap. There can be tax and convenience advantages, which help explain the recent rising popularity of share buybacks. Another cause is that if buybacks push up equity prices (there is some evidence in favor), they help keep executives' stock options above water. They can then cash them out, and purchase more options.

To examine capital gains and losses, we can differentiate the household balance sheet over time,

$$\dot{\Omega}_h = \dot{P}_e E + P_e \dot{E} + \dot{D}.$$

An increase in household wealth is made up of capital gains (if $\dot{P}_e > 0$), issues of new equity (if $\dot{E} > 0$) and new debt ($\dot{D} > 0$).

Substitution from the flow of funds (3.4) gives

$$\dot{\Omega}_h = S_h + \dot{P}_e E. \tag{3.6}$$

As discussed in Chapters 1 and 2, households become richer as a consequence of saving and capital gains (assuming $\dot{P}_e > 0$.)

---

[4] The Trump tax cuts of 2018 and 2019 provided another convenient source of funds.

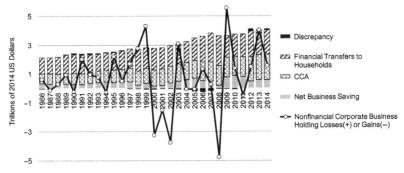

FIGURE 3.3   Business saving and holding losses

Firms, meanwhile, lose wealth as capital depreciates and equity prices rise,

$$\dot{\Omega}_b = S_b - \delta PK - \dot{P}eE. \tag{3.7}$$

The obvious empirical question is whether "holding losses" $-\dot{P}_eE$ for business exceed net saving $S_b - \delta PK$. Such losses are basically a paper transaction for business, but as noted, if $-\dot{P}_eE < 0$, the offsetting capital gain $\dot{P}_eE$ is real money for households.

Recall from the discussion of Figure 2.1 (macro level SAM for 2014), that business profits break down into financial transfers to households, taxes, CCA, and net saving, along with a "discrepancy" due to minor transfers. Figure 3.3 illustrates this decomposition over time. Overall, there is an upward trend in transfers to households. The discrepancy is small, and takes both signs. *Net* business saving is also "small" – well less than a trillion dollars per year. The question at hand is how does it compare to capital losses for business and gains for households?

In their "S" tables, the Federal Reserve and BEA publish estimates of business "holding losses" on outstanding liabilities, basically equity.[5] The solid line shows their levels over almost thirty years. The losses fluctuate over time, but pretty clearly they have exceeded net saving so there has been a transfer of wealth to

---

5   The losses are capital transfers from business to households. They are bookkeeping transactions for business but, as noted above, real money for households.

households. As illustrated in Figure 1.3, the main beneficiaries on a per household basis have been the top 1 percent. A related pattern shows up in the time path of levels of asset prices, the next topic at hand.

ASSET PRICE OF K

In his *General Theory* (1936) and even more in his *Treatise on Money* (1930), Keynes emphasized that the macroeconomy has two sets of prices – for goods and services on one hand and assets on the other. Insofar as it makes sense conceptually, aggregate capital K should have an asset price reflecting its expected returns. For better or worse, the stock market is supposed to signal the future path of corporate earnings. The riddle is how to gauge these returns for the purpose of understanding asset pricing.

Along with others, the American economist James Tobin (1969) proposed the *valuation ratio* $q = P_e E / P K$ as an appropriate asset price index (assuming that K can be approximated by perpetual inventory).[6] Figure 3.4 shows how q fits into rudimentary wealth accounting.

In contrast to (3.1), private sector wealth now sums to qPK,

$$\Omega_h + \Omega_b = qPK$$

Household wealth is still debt plus equity as in (3.2). In this simple balance sheet q would have to be substantially greater than 1 for business to have positive net worth. For $q = 1$,

	Capital	Equity	Debt	Net worth
Households		$P_e E$	D	Ω_h
Business	qPK	$-P_e E$	$-D$	Ω_b
Totals	qPK	0	0	qPK

FIGURE 3.4 Rudimentary wealth accounting with capital computed with a valuation ratio $q = P_e E / PK$ (in symbols)

[6] The basic idea of using a firm's stock market valuation to gauge its capital stock can be traced to Thorstein Veblen, Gunnar Myrdal, Maynard Keynes, Robin Marris, and Nicholas Kaldor (who called the ratio v).

$$\Omega_b = -D$$

The time patterns shown in Figure 3.3 suggest that $q > 1$ so that Ω_b, can take either sign. For a given level of q, if business runs up debt to buy back shares its nominal net worth could become negative.

CAPITALIZATION AND INTEREST RATES

As will be discussed in Chapter 5, q, in principle, should follow from long-term relationships between profit and real interest rates.[7] A quick and dirty approach called *capitalization* simply assumes that ρ, the *expected* return per unit time generated by a collection of capital goods, will stay constant, as will an "appropriate" real interest rate j (presumably provided by the market). Then one can use high school algebra to show that the return flow ρ discounted over time generates a value V_K of the capital goods collection given by

$$V_K = \rho/j \tag{3.8}$$

Because j is in the denominator, a lower value will be associated with a higher V_K. Over chronological time, the interest rate and asset prices appear to vary inversely. Did low rates contribute to rising household capital gains? It makes sense to take a look.

There are many factors driving interest rates. For the US economy, three can be noted here.

Recall that bond prices vary inversely with the interest rate. There has been a worldwide bond bull market – rising prices and falling rates – since the 1980s. Before that, rates in rich economies fluctuated in the range of 5 percent. They spiked to double digits with the Paul Volcker shock, and have been drifting downward ever since.

---

[7] The "real" interest rate is $j = i - \hat{P}$, with i as the nominal rate and $\hat{P}$ as the rate of price inflation for goods and services. According to Irving Fisher's "arbitrage" relationship, $r = i - \hat{P}$, the profit rate and real rate are supposed to move together. They do not, and if anything are negatively correlated (see figure 2.2 in Taylor, 2010, and Figure 3.6 here). Fisher arbitrage is another piece of irrelevant mainstream theory, but it features strongly in the Ramsey optimal saving model described in Chapter 5 in which the real interest rate (which determines asset price growth) and profit rate are assumed to be equal.

Given the high degree of integration in world capital markets, the USA has not been an exception.

Locally, beginning in the mid-1980s, the Federal Reserve cut interest rates after every stock market wobble (including the 1987 crash, the Mexican crisis, the Asian crisis, the Long-Term Capital Management collapse, the Y2K scare, the end of the Internet bubble, 9/11, and the 2008 financial crisis). From (3.8), we can see that keeping rates low must have supported asset prices. In Wall Street jargon, the Fed's Governor Alan Greenspan planted an interest rate "put" to shore up the stock market and aggregate demand. His successors Ben Bernanke, Janet Yellen, and Jerome Powell continued the practice.

Most importantly, as argued in the Introduction, wage repression is based on a declining growth rate of nominal unit labor cost. Because the price level is driven to a large extent by the money wage, inflation has dropped off. Interest rates have fallen in turn.

DETERMINATION OF q

In line with equation (3.8), the asset price q depends on the ratio of the profit rate to the real interest rate. Due at least in part to wage repression, the numerator has increased while the denominator has gone down.

Figure 3.5 illustrates how q has fared since World War II. Until the 1980s in the upper diagram, the levels of business fixed capital at current prices and the market value of corporate equities tracked fairly closely together, with equity a bit below capital. Since then, equity valuation has risen sharply, with a couple of booms and crashes. In the lower chart, q followed a similar pattern, rising from less than 0.5 in the 1970s to levels close to 2.0 in the late 1990s and 2010s. It may show a degree of "reversion to mean" but the pattern is not strong.

The period of the put began around in the early 1980s with the Mexican crisis and the reversal of the Volcker shock. To explore the effects on asset prices, let r^* stand for the ratio of business profits net of depreciation, taxes, and interest (illustrated

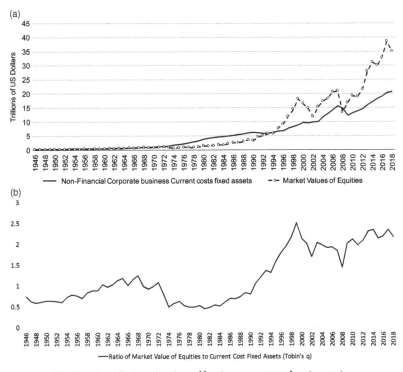

FIGURE 3.5 Determination of business sector valuation ratio q

in Figure 3.3) to real business capital. Then the (3.8) recipe for capitalization suggests that

$$q = r^*/j. \tag{3.9}$$

The upper chart in Figure 3.6 shows a decline in the real interest rate over nearly thirty-five years, accompanied by upward swings in the net profit rate. The lower chart compares observed q with r^*/j. The fit is by no means perfect, but both variables show a clear upward drift, interrupted by recessions. Despite the rough-and-ready nature of capitalization and the vagaries of the stock market, it seems clear that both growing profits and a falling interest rate contributed to rising asset prices and capital gains for the top 1 percent. Lagging wages were a major cause of both trends and the capital gains which flowed largely to the top 1 percent.

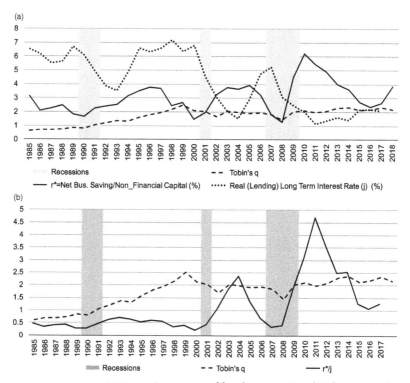

FIGURE 3.6 Net profit rate r^*, real lending rate j, and Tobin's q under the Greenspan-Bernanke-Yellen-Powell "put"

DATA ON WEALTH

Putting together time series on the distribution of wealth is not easy. As noted in Chapter 1, the share in wealth of the top 1 percent of households as estimated from expenditure survey or income tax data was around 50 percent just prior to the Great Depression, fell to 25 percent in the 1960s, and is now in the vicinity of 40 percent. Unsurprisingly, the valuation ratio in Figure 3.5 followed a somewhat similar trajectory.

Figure 3.7 is a snapshot of the contemporary distribution, based on data from the Federal Reserve's "S" tables. The Fed numbers include two kinds of capital – real estate and "other" which includes equipment – and several categories of financial claims, which are

2014 (in Trillions)	CAPITAL		Debt securities	Other financial assets	Equity and investment funds share	Net Worth
	Real Estate	Other				
All Households	23.67	0.32	3.06	19.00	32.93	78.97
Lower 60%	2.08	0.02	−0.32	−1.99	1.02	0.81
Middle 61–99%	15.37	0.16	2.51	15.61	9.96	43.60
Top 1%	6.22	0.15	0.86	5.38	21.95	34.56
Firms	21.67	7.78	−4.93	1.54	−19.80	6.26
Gov't	11.11	0.99	−16.04	−1.64	0.52	−5.05
Financial Business	1.03	0.57	10.55	−12.09	−1.10	−1.04
ROW	-		7.36	0.75	−2.42	5.69
Col.sum	57.48	9.67	0.00	7.55	10.13	84.83

DISAGGREGATION OF HOUSEHOLDS						
	REAL ESTATE SHARE	OTHER CAPITAL SHARE	DEBT SECURITIES SHARE	OTHER FINANCIAL ASSETS SHARE	EQUITY & INVESTMENT FUNDS SHARE	NET WORTH SHARE
Bottom 60%	8.79%	5.58%	−10.48%	−10.48%	3.10%	1.02%
61–99%	64.94%	48.44%	82.18%	82.18%	30.24%	55.22%
Top 1 %	26.26%	45.97%	28.30%	28.30%	66.67%	43.76%

FIGURE 3.7 US distribution of wealth, 2014

aggregated in the table. For each group of economic actors – households, firms producing goods and services, government, financial business, and rest of the world – assets have a positive sign and liabilities are negative. Net worth in the row for each group is the sum across columns. Total net worth is 84.8 (trillion dollars), of which 78.97 is held by households. GDP from Figure 2.1 is 17.35, giving a wealth/GDP ratio of 4.89 (well below numbers higher than 5 proposed by Piketty). Net worth of consolidated business is reported as positive (5.22) and government negative (−5.05). The rest of the world holds positive claims against the USA (mostly "debt securities" or bonds).

Total capital stock is 67.2, so the capital/GDP ratio is 3.87. This level is in the traditional range when capital is computed by perpetual inventory. If, say, capital is valued at an asset price qP with $q > 1.75$, as in the recent period, then the capital/GDP ratio would be 6.77, in the vicinity of Piketty. Presumably a big dose of "intangible capital" beyond what could be realized by selling corporations' real estate and machines in the market underlies the high value of q.

The columns for the three classes of financial claims – debt securities, other assets, and equity and investment funds – should each sum to zero. In fact they do not. Holdings of the latter two categories with positive signs down the columns are reported to exceed supplies with negative signs. At least the sign patterns make sense. Households hold "other" assets mostly issued by finance, and equity issued by business. The fact that the numbers are inconsistent by 18.65 trillion illustrates the difficulties of measuring wealth.

The configuration of wealth-holding in Figure 3.7 is not inevitable. Coming out of World War II and into the 1960s, American corporations had strongly positive net worth with capital estimated by perpetual inventory. Basically, they held a big stock of war-related government bonds. Till van Treeck (2015) points out that even today German business has positive net worth and explores the implications. Unsurprisingly in light of Figure 3.7's accounting, positive wealth in German business goes along with a low ratio of the value of equity to the capital stock or $q < 1$.

We allocated totals of household wealth to the three groups based on scrutiny of studies in the literature along with the distribution of capital gains across households.[8] The bottom 60 percent don't hold very much. The middle class owns real estate, other assets, and equity. The rich hold the same categories, with less emphasis on real estate and more on equity. Mean levels of net worth per household for the top 1 percent and middle class are $31.4 million and $1.02 million respectively.[9] Real estate makes up almost one-third of the wealth of the middle class.

SOCIAL VS. MARKET FORCES

Over time, regressive income redistribution in the medium run has extended to inequality of wealth. A rising profit share to the tune of

---

[8]   See Piketty, Saez, and Zucman (2016), Saez and Zucman (2015), and Wolff (2014).

[9]   Because of fat tails in the size distributions, these mean values undoubtedly exceed the medians.

many trillion dollars over two decades has been transferred through financial channels to households near the top of the income distribution. Their capital gains have been stimulated by lagging wages which boost the profit rate and reduce the interest rate. High savings rates and finance-based incomes have boosted inequality of wealth. Social and institutional forces driving these changes are discussed more in Chapter 5.

4 Sectoral Stagnation, Flat Productivity, and Lagging Real Wages

(coauthor Özlem Ömer)

This chapter analyzes changes in the structure of production, based on Karl Polanyi's ideas and insights by Arthur Lewis and a host of development economists. They postulated a natural transition of employment from a low-wage, low-productivity stagnant or subsistence zone to higher productivity industries or sectors, especially manufacturing. In fact, over twenty-five years this sort of transition has been running in reverse in the American economy.

Employment growth has been strong in sectors such as education and health, business services, and accommodation and food with low wages and productivity and slow productivity growth. Manufacturing has retained its traditional position as the main source of productivity growth, but its employment share is now less than 10 percent. Profits in real estate rental and leasing are high, but profit growth is concentrated in sectors with solid demand and productivity growth such as manufacturing, wholesale trade, and information.

In an old description from development economics, a "dual economy" in the USA has emerged, as pointed out by Temin (2015) and Storm (2017b). Using sectoral data since 1990 (when it became available), we show that the burden of sectoral stagnation mostly affected the middle class and, much more strongly, poorer households at the bottom of the size distribution of income. Households in the top 1 percent and higher, by contrast, benefitted because they get most of their income from steadily rising profits.

THE ROLE OF PRODUCTIVITY

How do production and distribution across industries, or "sectors," of the economy interact? Diagrams and numbers below show the evolution of sectoral levels and growth of real wages and labor productivity, the widely discussed ratio introduced in previous chapters,

Productivity = Real output/employment.

Productivity is an accounting relationship that links output, employment, and profits. It is tricky to apply because of complications to be discussed.[1] We then turn to shifts in intersectoral relative prices or the terms-of-trade between sectors. We propose an explanatory framework, drawing on insights from development economics and simple structuralist macro models.

In a common disaggregation, sixteen producing sectors are used to illustrate structural change. Compared to the others, seven have low levels of productivity, with growth rates of productivity and real wages lagging the rest. Their share of total employment rose from 47 percent in 1990 to 61 percent in 2016 while their share in wages went from 57 percent to 56 percent of the total. A stable wage share combined with rising employment demonstrates visible wage retardation. The sectors' real output share fell from 48 percent to 41 percent. This shift of labor toward low wage, low productivity jobs helps explain the striking increase of American income inequality.[2]

INCREASING IMBALANCES

Figure 4.1 begins to tell the tale. Productivity growth rates from 1990 to 2016 are displayed along the horizontal axis. The seven lagging sectors – construction, education and health along with other services (their two dots overlap), entertainment, accommodation and food,

1   In line with many national accountants' views, real output is measured as double-deflated chain-indexed value-added, with data from the US Bureau of Economic Analysis (BEA). Annual employment levels are provided by the Bureau of Labor Statistics (BLS). The ins and outs of double deflation and chain indexing are set out in Moyer et al. (2004) from the BEA. Other "real output" series go back in time beyond 1990.

2   Using longer time series for real outputs (not double deflated), Mendieta-Muñoz et al. (2019) show that divergence between static and dynamic sectors began after 1979.

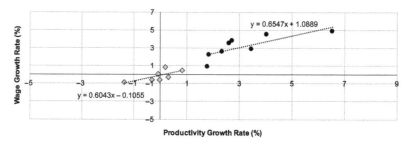

◇ Group 1 (Construction-Accom_Food-BusServices-Other Services-Edu_Health-Entertainment-Transport_Warehousing)

● Group 2 (Mining-Retail-Wholesale-Agriculture-Manufacturing-Utilities-Information-FI)

FIGURE 4.1 Productivity growth vs. product wage growth 1990–2016 (real estate and computer products sectors are not included)
Data Source: www.bea.gov/industry/gdpbyind-data
www.bls.gov/emp/tables/employment-by-major-industry-sector.htm

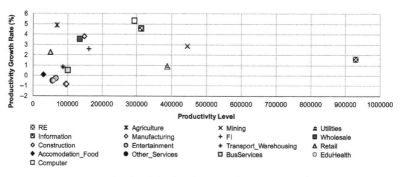

⊠ RE	✕ Agriculture	✕ Mining	⌂ Utilities
▨ Information	◇ Manufacturing	+ FI	▨ Wholesale
◇ Construction	○ Entertainment	✦ Transport_Warehousing	△ Retail
✦ Accomodation_Food	● Other_Services	⬚ BusServices	○ EduHealth
⬚ Computer			

FIGURE 4.2 Productivity levels vs. productivity growth rates, 1990–2016.
Source: www.bea.gov/industry/gdpbyind-data
www.bls.gov/emp/tables/employment-by-major-industry-sector.htm

business services, and transportation and warehousing – had rates hovering around 0 over the period from 1990 to 2016.

Figure 4.2 shows that these sectors, along with retail trade and agriculture, have productivity levels less than $100,000 per employed person per year (or roughly $55 per hour) in prices of 2009. Table 4.1 shows that the seven accounted for 46.8 percent of total employment in 1990 and 60.8 percent in 2016 – the proportion of down-market jobs shot up.

Table 4.1 *Summary data for the sectors*

SECTORS	PRODUCTIVITY GROWTH RATE (%)			REAL WAGE (per employee) GROWTH RATE (%)			REAL WAGE LEVEL (Total thousands of $)		EMPLOYMENT SHARE (%)		REAL WAGE SHARES IN TOTAL (%)		OUTPUT Growth (Current %)	OUTPUT Growth (Real %)
	INITIAL (1991)	FINAL (2016)	AVERAGE (1990–2016)	INITIAL (1991)	FINAL (2016)	AVERAGE (1990–2016)	INITIAL (1990)	FINAL (2016)	INITIAL (1990)	FINAL (2016)	INITIAL (1990)	FINAL (2016)	AVERAGE (1991–2016)	AVERAGE (1991–2016)
Computer and Electronic Products	18.46	5.30	17.36	10.88	5.70	16.11	3.41	146.12	2.02	0.84	0.16	2.15	3.91	15.06
Agriculture	-1.88	9.65	4.86	6.59	21.17	6.54	5.27	21.01	3.42	1.97	0.42	0.73	3.13	3.53
Information	0.57	4.01	4.54	-0.59	2.02	4.04	43.23	120.14	2.85	2.24	2.87	4.72	4.83	4.55
Manufacturing	1.96	0.36	3.80	2.53	1.31	2.72	36.17	72.07	18.76	9.92	15.76	12.51	2.95	2.43
Wholesale	5.12	-0.03	3.51	4.81	-0.01	2.61	40.97	78.52	5.58	4.70	5.31	6.47	4.59	3.72
Mining	5.65	2.47	2.87	19.86	8.92	3.45	96.00	148.51	0.81	0.54	1.81	1.39	5.74	2.36
FI	5.56	-3.88	2.60	0.31	-4.66	2.35	49.46	88.89	5.27	4.93	6.06	7.68	5.65	3.42
Retail	1.56	2.96	2.24	2.15	1.76	1.85	21.40	34.25	13.97	12.71	6.95	7.62	3.98	3.07
RE	0.54	1.60	1.60	-2.84	-2.14	1.01	45.62	58.83	1.74	1.72	1.84	1.77	5.00	2.51
Utilities	-3.00	4.42	0.91	-1.72	7.32	1.79	90.67	137.70	0.78	0.45	1.65	1.08	2.71	0.08
Transport_Warehousing	3.47	-2.02	0.80	2.40	-0.72	0.19	51.84	54.02	3.68	4.02	4.44	3.81	4.64	2.32
Business Services	-2.49	0.05	0.48	-0.94	-0.48	0.82	61.67	75.87	11.50	16.09	16.47	21.38	5.82	2.89
Accomodation & Food	-1.82	-1.71	0.05	-1.86	-2.47	-0.09	22.86	22.19	8.64	10.76	4.59	4.18	5.18	1.97
Entertainment	-5.57	-0.77	-0.31	-3.41	-0.71	0.30	38.67	41.48	1.20	1.81	1.08	1.31	5.45	2.46
Education & Health	-2.49	-0.68	-0.56	-2.47	-0.90	-0.31	55.82	51.47	11.69	18.17	15.15	16.37	5.61	2.26
Other Services	-1.91	-0.43	-0.56	-1.52	-1.32	-0.03	43.05	42.54	4.52	4.57	4.52	3.40	3.94	0.63
Construction	1.74	-0.76	-0.85	2.12	-0.71	-1.37	85.58	59.18	5.58	5.40	11.10	5.59	4.80	0.16

Growth rates of real wages are plotted along the vertical axis in Figure 4.1.[3] The rates for the bottom sectors were dismal – all less than 1 percent per year and four negative (see Table 4.1). The slope of a trend line through the points (or the cross-sectional elasticity of wage growth with respect to productivity growth) is 0.6. There was a substantial wage lag.

The other sectors have higher productivity levels and/or growth. As noted, retail and agriculture have relatively low productivity but respectable growth. Utilities have high productivity combined with slow growth. Finance and insurance (FI), manufacturing, wholesale, information, and mining have solid performances on both counts.

Real estate rental and leasing is peculiar. It has an exceptionally high own-profit share of value-added (over 90 percent) and measured productivity. The real estate business collects fees and rents, which flow into profits, but it does not create many jobs. It is basically an outlier. Computers and electronics comprise a sub-sector of manufacturing included to illustrate the properties of a relatively small but emerging leader of the economy (Houseman et al., 2014).

Ignoring real estate and computers, the trend line though the other sectors has a slope of 0.65. Bringing in the outliers gives a slope of 1.05. Either way, even the dynamic sectors demonstrate a lag of overall wage payments behind productivity. The fact that labor payments did not keep up with productivity across almost all sectors suggests that generalized wage suppression rather than price increases due to business monopoly was the key factor in making the income distribution become more unequal.[4]

A complicating factor is "induced innovation," a notion tracing at least to Marx and inserted into mainstream economics by Hicks (1932). The gist is that higher labor costs encourage firms to find ways

---

3   The growth rates refer to "product wages" or the costs of labor to business. They were estimated as current value wage shares of value-added times real labor productivity levels. The numbers are close to independent estimates of real wages. To give an example in round numbers, the end-of-period wage share in manufacturing was around 0.47. Productivity was $150,000, giving an average wage of $70,000 per employee.

4   See further discussion to follow and in Taylor and Ömer (2018a, 2018b).

to increase productivity. In the opposite direction, if business suc-
ceeds with wage suppression then there is less incentive for
productivity-increasing innovation. Along with other linkages we
will discuss, this feedback can worsen economic stagnation.[5]

Most dynamic sectors (but not agriculture and retail) had relatively high end-of-period wage levels. Shares of their wage payments
in the total typically exceeded their shares in employment. The opposite is true for the stagnant sectors, with business services (a mixed bag
of enterprises ranging from call centers through collection agencies to
credit bureaus and high-end management consulting, etc.) as the main
exception.

DUAL ECONOMY

Employment shares can be used to make a stab at estimating the size of
the dual economy. If more lucrative occupations from business services
are excluded from the 61 percent share of the seven sectors while low
wage workers in agriculture and retail trade are brought in, then, as
measured by employment, the size of the stagnant zone of the economy
might fall toward 50 percent – still a dismayingly high number.

There is also the question of the sizes of the shares of sectoral
value-added flows appropriated by the middle class (e.g., households
between the 61st and 99th percentiles of the size distribution who rely
largely on labor income) and the top 1 percent. Setting up
a spreadsheet showing how value-added by sector is distributed across
its payments to households is far beyond the scope of this book. But as
noted in Chapter 1, in prices of 2014 economy-wide mean labor compensation *per household* in the bottom 60 percent was in the range of
$30,000, below the estimates for the stagnant sectors of average wages
in prices of 2009 *per employee* in Table 4.1.[6] It appears that the bottom

[5]   Empirical work on "efficiency wage" models, popular before the turn of the century,
       suggested that a 10 percent decrease in the real wage might cut into productivity by
       5 percent.
[6]   As noted in Chapter 1, the mean for middle-class households is around $120,000 and
       over $500,000 for the top 1 percent. The share of unemployed persons in lower-income
       households (disproportionately female, minority, or young) is relatively high.

tier of households may well derive labor incomes from stagnant sectors in which wages are already low. Also, as we have noted, for the bottom 60 percent transfer income is almost as big as labor compensation.[7] If dualism is interpreted as referring only to household incomes, then one-third or more of recipients might be in the dual economy – still a very high proportion.

Tables 4.2a and 4.2b shed additional light on the duality question. As noted in prior chapters, sources of income for households include (i) labor compensation ("wages"); (ii) non-wage incomes including imputed rents on owner-occupied housing, proprietors' incomes, and depreciation; (iii) fiscal transfers; and (iv) interest and dividends paid via the financial sector.

Data on flows of household incomes at different levels generated by productive sectors are not readily available. Tables 4.2a and 4.2b present a *very* rough approximation for the three income strata used in previous chapters – the bottom 60 percent of households ("low"), households between the 61st and 99th percentiles ("middle"), and the top 1 percent ("high").

For the lower two groups, we split households between stagnant and dynamic sectors according to their different sources of incomes (not splitting the top group because it mainly relies on non-wage and financial incomes). We separated income from employment between sectors using the stagnant zone wage share mentioned. Non-wage income was split using the output share. The employment share was used for fiscal and financial transfers. The resulting macro-level flows in trillions of dollars in 2014 prices appear in Table 4.2a.

All the numbers are large, but differences among sectors and households already begin to appear. The top 1 percent do not receive significant fiscal transfers, while the bottom level households do.

---

[7]   In line with overall dualization of the economy, for the bottom three quintiles of the size distribution the ratio of government transfers to wage income rose from around one-third in the mid-1980s to near equality in the present decade. Most of this change was due to rising transfers while wage income grew slightly. As observed in Chapter 2, the middle class was squeezed between bigger transfers to low-income households and skyrocketing profits channeled to the top 1 percent.

Table 4.2a *Total household incomes by source and stagnant and dynamic sectors (trillions of 2014 dollars)*

Household	Wages		Non-wage		Transfers		Financial		Totals	
	Stagnant	Dynamic	Stagnant	Dynamic	Stagnant	Dynamic	Stagnant	Dynamic	Stagnant	Dynamic
Low	1.2	1	0.1	0.2	1	0.9	0.1	0.1	2.4	2.2
Middle	3.5	2.8	0.4	0.5	0.4	0.2	0.5	0.4	4.8	3.9
High	0.8		1.2		0.8		0.8		2.8	

Table 4.2b *Mean incomes per household by source and stagnant and dynamic sectors (thousands of 2014 dollars)*

Household	Wages		Non-wage		Transfers		Financial		Totals	
	Stagnant	Dynamic	Stagnant	Dynamic	Stagnant	Dynamic	Stagnant	Dynamic	Stagnant	Dynamic
Low	27	34	2	7	22	31	2	3	53	75
Middle	119	150	14	27	14	11	17	21	164	209
High	667		1000		667		667		2334	

Wage income for the middle group exceeds the flow to the bottom, and they also get visible incomes from other sources. Table 4.2b highlights these distinctions by presenting incomes per household.

The tables suggest that households in the lower income group who are active in the stagnant sector are visibly worse off than their counterparts in the dynamic zone. In other words, dualism shows up most strongly among the least well-to-do. The middle group is also subject to dualism, mainly in wage incomes. The top 1 percent is exempt. The wave of redistribution for the working classes shown in Table 4.1 did not reach higher income households that largely rely on proprietors' incomes and financial transfers generated by profits. Households in the stagnant zone were the hardest hit.

PRODUCTIVITY GROWTH

How did trends in productivity help produce this situation? Certainly the output/labor ratio is embedded within the overall socioeconomic system.[8] In practice, slower productivity and real wage growth may provide a vehicle for accommodating surplus labor coming from employment imbalances between stagnant and dynamic sectors. Following models proposed by Rada (2007) and Storm (2017b), we will see how productivity and wages adjust to employment imbalances.

There is another important consequence of productivity growth, not emphasized by mainstream economists. It creates an output "surplus" that must be distributed somehow to higher profits or wages. When real wages grow less rapidly than productivity, the share of profits in national income must rise. As pointed out in previous chapters, this process fuels the rapid growth of high household incomes that has occurred over the past several decades in the USA.

---

[8] For example, the "central dogma" of ecological economics is that the ratio of (mostly fossil fuel) energy use to employment rises in direct proportion to productivity (Semieniuk, 2018). Changing technology played a role but the entire means of production evolved to support this relationship.

"Value-added" is the standard metric for output. The numbers used in this study are subject to index number complications. As noted earlier, yearly levels of "real" value-added are estimated by "double deflation." A sector's gross output (including intermediate inputs) in current prices is deflated by an "appropriate" price index. The value of the intermediates deflated by another index is then subtracted to generate real value-added. Yearly estimates are strung together using a "chain index" (with varying weights over time) to produce a time series.[9]

Figure 4.3 shows how sectoral productivity levels evolved over time. Several points stand out, especially in light of recent debate discussed in Chapter 5 about the extent to which rising business monopoly power has led to more income inequality.

One observation is that aside from business services in panel B, the stagnant sectors are grouped in the low-productivity panels C and D. Along with business services, they show sluggish or negative productivity growth combined with rising employment. One is tempted to assume that holding down productivity was a means for business to create low-end, low-wage jobs for workers evicted from high productivity sectors. Productivity did rise in retail, a large low-wage employer. Its employment share fell as demand growth did not offset its productivity increases.

In the high productivity panel A, all four output/employment ratios grew. Real estate rental and leasing as noted above is an outlier. The utility and mining sectors are traditionally assumed to comprise firms with "natural" monopolies, while information has privileged access to data that it can exploit. In panel B, finance and insurance also

---

[9] In a bit more detail, a sector's total cost can be broken down into costs of intermediate inputs and value-added. Double deflation treats real value-added as a residual and so focuses on the interindustry structure of production. Current price estimates tend to estimate levels of output and value-added directly, making intermediate costs the residuals. Double deflation is less reliable for a sector when it is difficult to estimate the value of its output directly from market transactions. Simply adding up costs to determine output then becomes unavoidable. Education may be the most important example. It almost certainly has low productivity growth, but the estimate of –0.56 percent per year for education and health in Table 4.1 is imprecise.

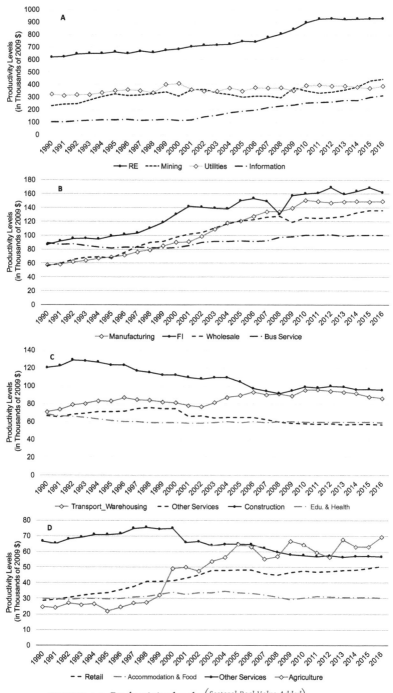

FIGURE 4.3 Productivity levels $\left(\frac{Sectoral\ Real\ Value\ Added}{Number\ of\ Employees}\right)$

Source: www.bea.gov/industry/gdpbyind-data

www.bls.gov/emp/tables/employment-by-major-industry-sector.htm

has monopoly elements. The diverse manufacturing sector has historically depended on continuing productivity growth; wholesale trade has benefitted from advances in inventory control.

The bottom line, perhaps, is that productivity increases may have gone along with monopoly power in dynamic sectors (and some subsectors). Productivity growth did *not* accelerate, suggesting that any increases in monopoly power did not play a role (see the discussion of "superstar" firms in Chapter 5). In panels C and D, employment increases may provide a better explanation than monopoly for slow or negative productivity growth and the wage lag.

Across the sixteen sectors, overall productivity growth can be decomposed into a weighted average of own-rates of increase and "reallocation" effects due to labor movements.[10] For instance, an increase in employment in a low productivity sector reduces economy-wide productivity growth.

Figure 4.4 presents the sectoral contributions. Toward the right, job growth in education and health and accommodation and food cuts

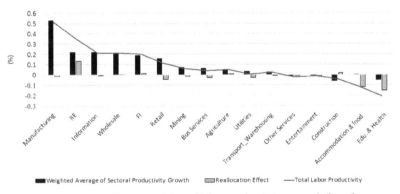

FIGURE 4.4 Decomposition of labor productivity growth (based on double-deflated output levels)
Source: www.bea.gov/industry/gdpbyind-data
www.bls.gov/emp/tables/employment-by-major-industry-sector.htm

10   The weights are sectoral shares in output for productivity growth and differences between output and employment shares for growth of employment. If its output share exceeds its employment share, a sector has relatively high productivity so that if its employment rises there is a positive contribution to overall productivity growth.

visibly into overall productivity. Toward the left, real estate and manufacturing have real output shares in the range of 12–15 percent and make strong productivity contributions. Shares of finance and insurance, retail, wholesale, and information cluster above 5 percent. Table 4.1 shows that all these sectors had visible own-productivity growth, explaining the pattern in Figure 4.4. Business services is a large sector at around 15 percent but its slow own-productivity growth means that it did not contribute very much economy-wide.

EMPLOYMENT GROWTH

Productivity shifts provide a means to explore movements in overall employment. At the aggregate level, it is true that

$$\text{Employment/Population} = (\text{Output/Population}) / (\text{Output/Employment})$$

or

$$\text{Employment ratio} = \text{Output per capita/Productivity}$$

This formula provides the basis for a decomposition of growth in the employment ratio over time as a weighted average of growth rates of sectoral outputs per capita minus growth rates of productivity. The weights are sectoral employment shares. Using working age population for convenience, Figure 4.5a presents the results.

In the relatively large manufacturing sector, productivity growth outstripped demand growth, so jobs were destroyed. There was a rough balance in the other sectors toward the left. Demand growth along with stagnant productivity led to job creation in business services and accommodation and food. Both demand expansion and falling productivity pushed up employment in education and health.

Figure 4.5b shows the combined effects on the employment ratio of output and productivity changes. The bulk of job creation took place in the seven sectors pointed out previously (and grouped toward the bottom of Table 4.1). In increasing order, job annihilation took place in information, wholesale, retail, agriculture, and

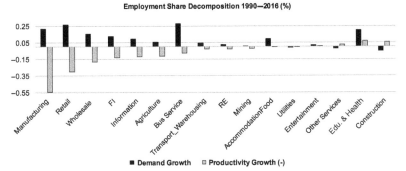

FIGURE 4.5A Employment share decomposition
Source: www.bea.gov/industry/gdpbyind-data
www.bls.gov/emp/tables/employment-by-major-industry-sector.htm
https://fred.stlouisfed.org/series/LNS12034560

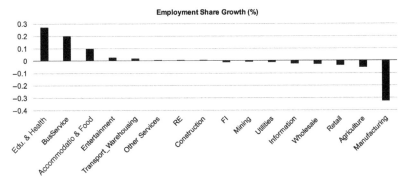

FIGURE 4.5B Employment share growth (demand growth + productivity
growth from Figure 4.4)
Source: www.bea.gov/industry/gdpbyind-data
www.bls.gov/emp/tables/employment-by-major-industry-sector.htm
https://fred.stlouisfed.org/series/LNS12034560

manufacturing. Robotization, the latest manifestation of the trend
toward automation that has run for more than two centuries, no
doubt contributed to slower job growth, mostly by blocking young
entrants into the industrial labor force.

Notably, there are thirty-six weekly employment hours for business services; education and health, thirty-three; and accommodation

and food, twenty-six. Manufacturing has forty-one weekly hours. In effect, jobs shifted toward sectors with both low wages and short hours.[11]

PROFIT SHARE GROWTH

Five decades of steady growth of the profit share have already been demonstrated in Figure I.1. An immediate question regards the sectors in which it originated. In terms of levels, four sectors provide close to one-third of total value-added along with substantial profits – real estate (14 percent), manufacturing (8 percent) and finance-insurance and business services (4 percent each). They are followed by information (3.5 percent), wholesale (2.5 percent), and retail and construction (2 percent each).[12]

Levels of profits say nothing about where growth came from. The profit share is equal to 1 minus the wage share, which in turn is the ratio of the real wage to productivity. This accounting provides the basis for a decomposition like the ones already discussed. The growth rate of the profit share economy-wide is a weighted average of productivity (+), wages (-) and a demand shift effect (±). Figure 4.6 shows the results.

Effects of demand shifts were relatively minor, but they did stimulate profits arising in information, wholesale and retail trade, and finance-insurance. Along with manufacturing (strong productivity growth and visibly lagging wages), these sectors played the major roles in driving economy-wide profits. Among minor contributions, construction suffered from a demand shift and falling productivity, but benefitted from falling real wages. Business services had relatively strong wage increases. Notably, despite its high levels of profits and productivity, the contribution of the real estate sector to profit share growth was negligible.

---

[11]　One might add "and multiple jobs." According to BLS data, about 5 percent of US workers hold more than one job, with the share apparently declining. See https://fred .stlouisfed.org/series/LNS12026620.

[12]　See Taylor and Ömer (2018) for the rest of the list.

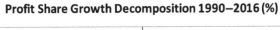

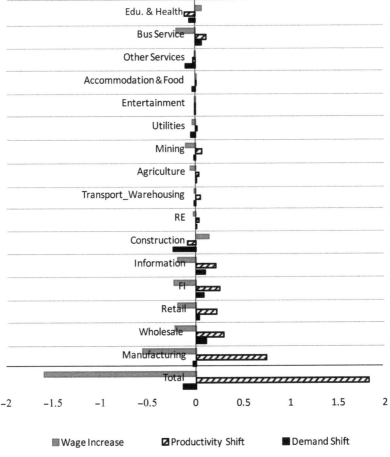

FIGURE 4.6 Profit share growth decomposition

TERMS OF TRADE

As discussed, "real" output levels are calculated by deflating production flows at market values by price indexes. With this methodology in action, the signal that a sector is enjoying relatively high productivity growth is that the current price value of its real output is falling relative to the rest of the economy. In other words, its "terms of trade" are deteriorating. The terms of trade will shift in favor of a sector with lagging productivity in line with the "Baumol effect" (Baumol and Bowen, 1966).[13] Computer power has become relatively less expensive over time while the cost of health care has gone up.

The last column of Table 4.1 shows sectoral growth rates of double-deflated, chain-indexed output. One immediate observation is that manufacturing grew less rapidly than other sectors (e.g., its own computer and electronics subsector), information, wholesale and retail trade, and finance and insurance. Slower output growth in manufacturing is to be expected in light of historical experience in countries at all income levels worldwide.[14]

Sectoral real growth rates can be compared to the rates shown in the second-last column, which were calculated by deflating value-added in current prices by an overall price index called the GDP deflator. *Differences* between the two columns reflect productivity trends. The lagging seven sectors at the bottom of the table all had (deflated) current price growth rates that exceeded their real rates so that prices shifted in their favor. With a few exceptions, the opposite is true of the dynamic sectors. The 12 percent growth rate differential or relative price decrease for computers is particularly striking.[15]

---

13   The "effect" is often interpreted as stating that real wages tend to rise in industries with slow productivity growth, pushing up costs. For the data summarized in Table 4.1, this version of Baumol's idea is not true. It can be rejected on accounting grounds. The real (product) wage equals labor productivity times the wage share. Such shares are relatively stable so that growth of the wage will be roughly proportional to growth of productivity. The fact that in Table 4.1 wages lag productivity in low end sectors means that their profits have benefitted most from Baumol effects.

14   In Europe, for example, according to World Bank data, the manufacturing share of real GDP in Germany fell from 25 percent in 1991 to 21 percent in 2017, and in Sweden from 21 percent in 1980 to 14 percent in 2016. The decrease in the USA was from 16 percent in 1997 to 12 percent in 2016.

15   On the assumption that prices are largely driven by labor costs, the older literature on international trade traced shifts in the "double factorial terms of trade" to differences between wage growth minus productivity growth across countries. In the current context, if wage growth rates are equal, a *negative* difference of this indicator between dynamic and stagnant sectors arises if productivity growth is higher in the former than the latter (as in Table 4.1). That is, prices shift against the dynamic sectors due to productivity growth differentials.

STAGNANT AND DYNAMIC SECTORS

The evidence shows that the seven sectors toward the bottom of Table 4.1 fall behind in labor income, profits, and output while creating employment. The ones toward the top of the table have high and rising productivity, albeit with real wage suppression. The question is how dynamic and stagnant sectors interact.

Both Storm (2017b) and Rada (2007) assume that workers who do not find dynamic sector jobs are driven into the stagnant part of the economy. To paraphrase Storm: for rich economies, especially the USA, this "full employment" assumption reflects the fact that, in the absence of unemployment insurance and social security worth the name, workers must find jobs, if not in the better paid core, then in a low-end job in some peripheral activity. In contrast to standard models, endogenous adjustment of productivity in the stagnant sector allows employment (supplemented by fiscal transfers) to be maintained

This idea traces back to debates in development economics a half-century ago when Lewis proposed that poor countries have "surplus labor" (or a "reserve army" in Marx's terminology), which can be brought from subsistence activity into employment in an expanding modern sector. Sen (1966) pointed out that subsistence output would change very little as labor moved in and out of the sector. In effect, he suggested that productivity would *fall* in proportion to the quantity of labor moving *into* the sector, or that the elasticity of productivity with respect to employment equals minus 1, in a strong case of decreasing returns. A microeconomic rationale is that as subsistence employment increases, the real wage will fall. In line with the induced innovation hypothesis discussed above, productivity growth would slow. Slow productivity increases in the face of rising employment for the stagnant sectors in Table 4.1 suggests that this idea continues to apply today, although the magnitude of the relevant (negative) "Sen elasticity" would be difficult to quantify.[16]

---

[16] For activities like education and health, growth of real wages and productivity might decrease more than in proportion to increasing employment,

Another model originally proposed in the 1960s and published by Kaldor (1978) suggests that, in the dynamic part of the economy, the growth rate of productivity may respond positively to the growth rate of output. Can this linkage create jobs?

To answer the question, we have to look at the impacts of a productivity increase at an initial level of output. Because

Unit labor cost = Real wage/Productivity,

labor becomes cheaper, pushing up profits and stimulating investment as well as making exports more competitive. Via both channels, aggregate demand may rise.

At the same time, because

Employment = Output/Productivity,

jobs are destroyed and labor income falls, reducing consumption demand. In the jargon, if higher investment and exports more than offset lower consumption, the economy is said to be "profit-led"; otherwise it is "wage-led." Two further points:

(i)   The final outcome may generate *more* jobs than before the productivity increase *if* the system is "strongly" profit-led.[17] Employment will definitely decrease when demand is wage-led.

(ii) As underlined in Chapter 1, US expenditure survey data suggest that savings rates are negative for low-income households, which rely roughly half-and-half on wage and transfer income. If the income shift from wages to profits mostly damages middle-class households (with, say, higher than median incomes mostly coming from wages), then, as shown formally in Chapter 5, aggregate demand may be both profit- and low income-led.

Whether the US economy is wage or profit-led is controversial.[18] But it surely is not strongly enough profit-led for a productivity increase to raise employment. In other words, faster productivity growth in the

---

[17]   The formal condition is that the elasticity of aggregate demand with respect to the inverse of unit labor cost should exceed 1, which is not likely to be satisfied.

[18]   Debate about which response dominates was set off by Rowthorn (1982) and Dutt (1984) and has continued endlessly ever since. Bhaduri and Marglin (1990) is an influential (now somewhat dated) summary.

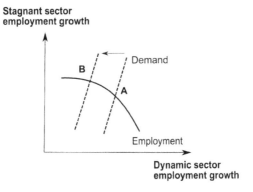

FIGURE 4.7 Effects of an upward shift of productivity growth when the dynamic sector is not strongly profit-led

dynamic sector forces workers to move to the stagnant zone in which firms adjust by using more workers to produce the same real output.

The next question is how strong are feedbacks from the stagnant to dynamic sectors? Figure 4.7 illustrates.

The "Employment" schedule shows that a change in the growth rate of dynamic sector employment must be met by an offsetting shift in the growth of stagnant sector jobs (the slope depends on employment shares). The system must adjust along the schedule on the full employment assumption.

The "Demand" curve shows how strongly income generated by faster growth of stagnant sector jobs stimulates employment growth in the dynamic sector. The Sen elasticity and the response of stagnant sector real wages to productivity both affect this response. The schedule may be steep if there is relatively weak feedback of stagnant sector employment onto demand for dynamic sector goods and services.

A jump in dynamic sector productivity growth shifts the demand schedule to the left, moving the economy from point A to point B. Employment is pushed into the stagnant sector, forcing down productivity there. The initial sectoral imbalance gets worse. As employment is pushed out of the dynamic sector, moreover, demand generated by low-wage workers in the stagnant zone will drop off and the schedule may shift further to the left. This movement itself can be a major source of secular stagnation.

SOCIAL VS. MARKET FORCES

Output, employment, and income flows in the American economy fell apart over recent decades. Market forces – productivity and demand growth – were certainly involved. A "dual economy" emerged, signaled by divergence between "stagnant" and "dynamic" sectors in the structure of production, growing employment in stagnant industries, and rapidly rising inequality in the functional and size distributions of income. These imbalances mostly affected the middle class and, much more strongly, poorer households at the bottom of the size distribution. Households in the top 1 percent and higher thrived because they get most of their income from steadily rising profits.

A key aspect of the process was lagging productivity growth in the stagnant sectors. Here, social factors may have been involved, as jobs were created to take advantage of workers expelled from the dynamic zone of the economy, especially manufacturing.

5   Institutions and Models for Maldistribution

Chapter 6 presents simulation results from a simple, demand-driven economic growth and distribution model based on the numbers we have discussed. This chapter provides background for the simulations. It first takes up proposed institutional explanations for increasing income inequality, with regard to labor market power, then forces supporting high profits and wealth, and implications of duality. The second part of the chapter summarizes aspects of demand-driven macroeconomics as it is influenced by distribution. Relevant algebra is presented in the Appendix.

EXPLAINING THE FINDINGS ABOUT WAGES

There is ongoing tension between market-based and political economy explanations for trends in bargaining power. Mainstream economists of course prefer the former. As emphasized in the Introduction, the strength of the methodology developed here is that consistent accounting is imposed on the data at the macro and (in Chapter 4) "meso" levels. More orthodox analysis tends to begin with microeconomics and then extrapolate to the macro; so to speak, from the trees to the forest.

Nelson Barbosa (2019) points to important political economy factors affecting wage income for most workers. One is change in institutional norms: laws, unionization, and other informal rules of the game. Robert Solow (2015), who proposed the central orthodox economic growth model more than sixty years ago, engaged in the Cambridge controversies from the MIT side, and is now the doyen of mainstream macroeconomics, observes that labor suffered for several reasons. "The decay of unions and collective bargaining, the explicit hardening of business attitudes, the popularity of right-to-work laws, and the fact that the wage lag seems to have begun at about the same time as the Reagan presidency," Solow says, "all point in the same direction: the share of wages in national value added may have fallen because the social bargaining power of labor has diminished."

Falling or stable wages are exacerbated by nonpoaching and noncompetition clauses in labor contracts, which restrict job opportunities outside a company for a worker who leaves it. These exemplify divide-and-rule employment tactics in a "fissuring" market (Weil, 2014). The "gig" economy is another manifestation. In a review of the data, Abraham et al. (2018) suggest that gig workers make up 8 to 10 percent of the labor force, trending slightly downward (according to Census data) or upward (based on income tax self-employment earnings).

A complementary, more orthodox microeconomic interpretation is that business *monopsony* (or single buyer) power has grown stronger in the labor market. The overlap with mainstream "monopoly" explanations for high profits, as we will discuss, is striking. Microeconomics traditionally focuses on "agents" who take prices as given or subject to a degree of local control. But agents on one side of a market may confront those on the other who lack socially embedded bargaining power as in Solow's description. Expansion of free markets, or laissez-faire, cuts directly into labor's bargaining position. The Great Recession and a general acceptance of austerity to hold down barely visible inflation as a desirable policy goal have surely been recent contributing factors as well.

Technological change also plays a role. As noted in Chapter 4, the theory of induced innovation suggests that cost-cutting by firms will concentrate on inputs into production with high shares in total cost. Labor has the highest share by far. The standard implication is that firms will pursue labor productivity increases subject to an "invention possibility frontier."[1]

---

[1]   See Foley et al. (2019), chapter 7.

Besides increasing productivity, firms with labor market power can reduce costs by wage repression, presumably subject to an "exploitation possibility frontier." Productivity might well decline. The impact on unit labor cost (as noted previously, the ratio of the real wage to productivity) could go either way, but could well be negative, as in Chapter 4's Rada-Storm model. Institutional changes, which reduce labor's bargaining power, effectively mean that the exploitation frontier shifted "downward" after 1980, allowing more aggressive wage repression to be pursued. All these maneuvers become more tempting for business if full employment policy is not pursued at the macro level.

International trade came to the political forefront in the 2016 Presidential election. The issue is contentious, but recent work, for example, that by Autor, Dorn, and Hanson (2013), suggests that perhaps one-quarter of job loss in US manufacturing can be explained by import competition. It bears note, however, that manufacturing provides less than 10 percent of total employment.

Chapter 4 shows that overall productivity growth largely originates in manufacturing, but that employment is generated in sectors with relatively low wages. Meanwhile the pattern of demand switches toward them. The key to a tighter labor market in a sector and economy-wide is the difference between growth of demand per capita and labor productivity growth. Recently in the American economy, there has been increasing dualism between low productivity, high employment "stagnant" sectors and "dynamic" sectors with more rapid productivity increases but lagging real wage growth. Wages and productivity both slow down in a destabilizing feedback loop.

RISING PROFITS

What explains the rising profit share and payments from profits to upper-income households, implicit in Figure 1.4? The expansion of free market thinking has supported significant changes in institutional norms (laws and non-formal rules of the game) that shape business behavior. Lazonick (2014) points out that the stage for enhanced exploitation was set by the now-entrenched ideology that the unique goal of business should be to maximize shareholder value of firms. Massive buybacks and rising equity prices have been the major consequence, to the detriment of capital formation, wages of ordinary workers, employment, and the quality of goods and services provided in the market.

On the regulatory front, antitrust has shifted from an overall concern about the ill effects of corporate behavior as exemplified by trustbusters Theodore Roosevelt and Louis Brandeis toward an exclusive fixation on price-gouging, following the same Chicago-style economics that gave rise to maximizing shareholder value (Wu, 2018). As illustrated in Figure I.1, this reversal of New Deal antitrust was associated with deteriorating economic performance (Glick, 2019).

Harnessing the power of platform companies like Facebook and Google does not blend well into 2019 regulatory concerns. There is also little emphasis on constraining vertical integration, a strategy pursued by Amazon and Apple. Nevertheless, there are proposals on the table. Three are (i) restricting entry by existing platform companies into other markets (e.g., transport and financial services); (ii) pulling the companies apart to reduce cross-subsidization (e.g., Google's support of Gmail and Maps by search advertising revenue); and (iii) reversing past acquisitions such as Google's purchase of YouTube or Facebook's acquisition of WhatsApp.

Another contemporary issue is tariffs. In the early days of trust-busting, there was a major push to take away tariffs protecting entrenched industries, such as sugar. Will a new era of protectionism re-erect similar barriers?

These questions are for the future. Mainstream analysts rationalize high profits by pointing to enhanced monopoly power of business in markets for goods and services (Furman and Orzag, 2015). Certainly, enterprise concentration across the economy has risen. The platform companies are obvious examples, although the information and relevant subsectors of retail generate well less than 5 percent of employment and 10 percent of output.

In a recent widely discussed idea, an expanding presence of "superstar" firms with high productivity may drive down the average sectoral wage share (Autor et al., 2017). In Figure 4.3, the observation that productivity did not accelerate in dynamic sectors points away from this interpretation. Moreover, any such account requires an explanation of the institutional barriers that prevent workers in super firms from getting higher pay. We get back to wage repression.

The real question is whether pushing up prices against wages through monopoly power or driving down wages against prices through monopsony is the more important contributor to the rising profit share. Any attempt at quantification would be driven by the details of the model used, but the analysis in this study shows that conventional accounts that in effect rely on only one blade of the wage scissors cannot be anything like the whole story

WEALTH INEQUALITY

Income growth and wealth accumulation commingle, especially at the top. Linkages are worth exploring.

For example, mainstream microeconomics sees the dynamics of the valuation ratio q (Figure 3.6) as arising from market positions that generate "excess" profits. As in Chapter 3, a recent argument asserts that a positive difference since around 2000 between the corporate profit rate and the real interest rate creates a surplus that gets transferred to shareholders via capital gains (Eggertsson et al., 2018). Wage repression and the Federal Reserve put make this scenario plausible.

On the other hand, under different institutions there is no reason to assume that the wedge of profit over interest rates will persist; just recall the Volcker interest rate hike around 1980 and the relatively high rates in the decades before the bond market boom. Rate differentials, moreover, are irrelevant to the gap between real wage and productivity growth emphasized throughout this book. Based on the savings and investment flows discussed in Chapter 2, one might add that the mainstream idea that the "natural" interest rate has shifted downward permanently makes no institutional sense

(Taylor, 2017). The natural rate idea is based on loanable funds interest theory, which is refuted below.

Another popular view is that, at least in part, concentration of wealth stems from higher rents. For well over two centuries, rent has been understood as a payment for the use of some asset. In other words it originates from its owner's monopoly position, supported by law and threat of coercion, legally sanctioned or otherwise, if payments are not forthcoming. But rent will not arise if demand for the asset's services does not exist.

As described in Chapter 4, the real estate rental and leasing sector generates a quarter of total profits, estimated in the NIPA system on the basis of market transactions along with an "imputed" income flow for owner-occupied housing. Piketty (2014), Stiglitz (2016), and Furman and Orzag (2015) point to capitalized rents as a significant source of wealth inequality. But, as shown in Figure 4.6, real estate does not contribute to *growth* of profits. Regardless, the rent argument is worth pursuing briefly.

The conditions that give rise to rent are often left unstated. One is that simple scarcity of some input into production – say agricultural land or oil in the ground – or consumption – say housing – can give rise to nonzero payments from users to owners of the scarce resource. Since the days of Adam Smith and David Ricardo, it has been recognized that levels of these payments will ultimately be determined by users' incomes, as well as their microeconomic price elasticities of demand.

Second, "rent-seeking" (Anne Krueger, 1974) is a favored vehicle for mainstream economists to bring class and power into discussion. Rents become claims on income associated with sociopolitical relationships, which do not themselves create income. For example, a firm bribes politicians to get legislation increasing its profits. This version was popularized by Gordon Tullock (1967). Even he, however, emphasized difficulties in identifying rent-creating claims.

In a more recent variant from the Chicago Business School, Rajan and Zingales (2004) say that deregulating financial markets subject to proper government control in developing economies will make local capitalists relinquish rent-controlling positions that they have built up. The argument is a twist on the old development economics notion that getting rid of "financial repression" will supercharge growth (e.g., McKinnnon, 1973, and Shaw, 1973). It has never been convincing, and Rajan and Zingales add no force.

Finally, market power per se can move prices away from the values that would be observed in a "competitive" situation. This form of rent is the standard neoclassical version of exploitation. Any monopoly or monopsony position is the artifact of the social and institutional structures in place at the time. Over the past few decades they have shifted in favor of capital, with visible consequences.

Rents, legitimate or not, become sources of wealth inequality if they are capitalized. The crucial question is how they can be measured. They are payment flows *within* the macro system – money changes hands. In principle, they should show up in the national accounts. Real estate (or "land" in Stiglitz's usage) is the obvious example. Profits before depreciation, taxes, and interest in that sector are on the order of 3 trillion dollars. If they are capitalized to 5 percent (a plausible value in terms of Figure 3.6), the resulting value of capital in real estate would be $60 trillion, not far from the level in Figure 3.7.

In sum, real estate profits do not appear to be a major cause of rising concentration of income or wealth. The sky-high housing costs in Manhattan, the Bay Area, Mayfair, and similar hot spots reflect local purchasing power, much of it originating from abroad. They feed back into inequality, but, by themselves, are not the primary cause. Similar observations apply to rents on other sources such as agricultural land or mineral extraction rights. They arise in small corners of the economy and are driven by demand from elsewhere.

Finally, Stiglitz sees rents on intangible capital and rent-seeking as the major sources of incomes at the very top of the distribution, a market-based spin on a profound shift in the social contract between labor and capital. Lazonick (2015) attributes this change to the joint unequalizing effects of business "rationalization," "marketization," and "globalization," partially reflected in the rising labor compensation of rich households shown in Figures 1.4 and 1.5.

One anecdote is illuminating. The head of the Norway's energy company Equinor (until recently, Statoil) gets less than 2 million US dollars per year in his pay package. The CEO at ConocoPhillips, a comparably sized American company, receives more than ten times as much. Presumably both gentlemen are competent at their jobs; so, why is the American paid so much more? His "marginal product," whatever that means, cannot be *that* much bigger.

The Norwegian's relative penury is a consequence of the Nordic socioeconomic model, which has rested for decades on income equalization. The United States was never anywhere near as egalitarian as Norway; but, it is striking how its societal tolerance for enormous payments to people at the top has grown over the past three decades. That social decision could be reversed.

IMPLICATIONS OF DUALITY

In terms of "policy" as usually interpreted, the simulation results in Chapter 6 show that there is a limited menu of interventions that can be used to combat inequality. One could be based on fiscal or monetary expansion to push up demand for dynamic sector goods and services, pulling jobs from the stagnant sectors. The practical problem is that, although among policy-makers faith in "expansionary austerity" may be weakening, it has certainly not disappeared.

As shown later in this chapter, policies aimed at redistributing income toward the lower deciles of the size distribution in which households have negative saving rates would have a similar effect. An increase in fiscal transfers to low-income households over recent decades no doubt supported effective demand. The recent Trump tax "reform" of course went in the opposite direction.

Income policies could be used to stimulate wage growth in stagnant sectors relative to increases in the dynamic part of the economy.

These and similar adjustments could be helpful but fail to address more fundamental structural problems. The low positive or negative productivity growth in the dysfunctional American health care system is devastating. Employment in manufacturing, historically the main locus of productivity growth, will probably remain weak. Income elasticities of demand for the whole range of manufactured final goods (or "stuff") and even intermediates are not likely to rebound even as productivity growth continues.

Globalization and international trade have taken a toll in terms of jobs, not only in manufacturing. Offshoring the production of intermediate inputs, ranging from computer code to reading mammograms, cuts costs and raises the productivity of remaining workers in the USA. Creative destruction of onshore jobs still *is* destruction. Its impact may be stronger if investment in new technologies shifts from the USA to abroad.

Strong forces embedded in the economy support the trend toward duality. Distributive conflict lies at the root. It can be addressed from several angles: (i) revamped corporate governance, as in proposals from Senator Elisabeth Warren and others; (ii) restructured labor market regulation to give workers more bargaining power; and (iii) even capital market innovations, such as creation of a public wealth fund based on taxation of capital gains. Stagnation may well worsen unless a new double movement à la Polanyi brings these countervailing powers into play. Active macro policy would have to play a role.

MODELING MACROECONOMIC INEQUALITY

Next we turn to more formal models of key aspects of macroeconomic inequality. The first topic is short- to medium-run interaction between income distribution and demand, followed by a discussion of the dynamics of capital and wealth. Next come asset prices and the interest rate. There is a brief critique of mainstream ideas about determination of the interest rate, followed by observations on "secular stagnation," a 2019 macroeconomic topic du jour (Summers, 2015;

Storm, 2017b; Taylor, 2017). The main text is an attempt to use words to explain the models, and there is algebra in the Appendix.

EFFECTS OF DISTRIBUTION ON AGGREGATE DEMAND

Since the 1980s, there has been active debate about whether aggregate demand is "wage-led" or "profit-led," already discussed in Chapters 2 and 4. The rate of saving from profit income exceeds the rate from wages; so, a distributive shift toward the latter should stimulate consumption. On the other hand, lower profits may retard capital formation and exports, reducing demand overall (recall the various components of demand in the first rows of the SAMs in Figures 2.1 and 2.2).

Empirical results are mixed. Econometrics based on two-dimensional dynamical demand versus distribution systems points to profit-led demand in the USA and other rich countries. There is also strong evidence for a "profit squeeze" due to rising real wages as employment and output rise. The two relationships together determine the profit share and aggregate demand.[2] Single-equation estimation results often are interpreted to say that demand is wage-led because they report a positive relationship between output and the labor share. But then you never know whether a demand or distribution curve is being estimated. The latter seems more statistically robust. In the jargon, a single equation has an "identification problem" because it doesn't know which relationship it is supposed to represent.

The fact, emphasized in previous chapters, that lower-income households may have *negative* saving rates adds a further twist because the distributional distinction between low and high wages comes into play. Demand may be *both* profit- *and* "low income-led."[3] To see why, suppose that total income is split three ways, flowing to profits, middle-class households with relatively high wages, and low-wage earners. The

---

2   For econometric applications, see Barbosa-Filho and Taylor (2006) and Kiefer and Rada (2015). Implications for the business cycle will be discussed.

3   Carvalho and Rezai (2016) emphasize the latter linkage.

shares of these income flows in the total must sum to 1. Saving rates from profits and higher wage incomes are positive.

In a thought experiment, suppose that the profit share rises. The increase is met by an offsetting fall in the low wage share while the share of the middle class stays constant. In a profit-led system, investment will rise. The spending rate from low incomes exceeds 100 percent, on the other hand, so that consumption will decrease. Aggregate demand could move either way.

To work out the implications, let Δ be the inverse of the familiar Keynesian multiplier $1/\Delta$ (i.e., an increase in Δ forces aggregate demand to fall). Using parameters from the Appendix, consider a "small" increase in the income share of profits combined with a decrease of the same amount in the share of the poor. If the saving rate s_π from profit income is 0.6 and the coefficient for the effect of the profit rate on investment is $\alpha_r = 0.7$, then the net demand stimulus would make Δ drop in inverse proportion to $\alpha_r - s_\pi = 0.1$, raising output. With a saving rate of -0.2, the decrease in the low-income share ψ_p would boost Δ in inverse proportion by 0.2. The net effect from the back of this envelope is that the consumption loss would exceed the net investment gain by 0.1, reducing $1/\Delta$ and forcing output to decline in a low income–led economy.

These results inform the simulation model in Chapter 6, in which transfers from the top 1 percent to the bottom 60 percent stimulate demand, as do wage increases at the bottom.

EFFECTS OF OUTPUT AND EMPLOYMENT ON DISTRIBUTION

How do the level of economic activity and distribution interact in the short to medium run? Karl Marx threw light on distribution. In several passages in *Capital*, he sketched a theory of business cycles (a century later formalized by the American-born Cambridge economist Richard Goodwin, 1967) pivoting on class conflict. At the bottom of a cycle, the real wage ω is held down by a large reserve army of un- or underemployed workers, and capitalists can accumulate freely. However, as

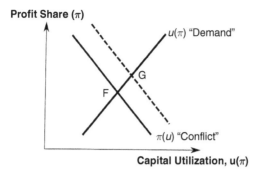

FIGURE 5.1 Determination of the profit share π and capital utilization u. The dashed line shows the effect of an upward drift in the profit share.

output expands, the reserve army is depleted as capital utilization u goes up. The real wage rises in response to a tighter labor market, forcing a profit squeeze. The "Conflict" schedule in Figure 5.1 underlies this cyclical linkage from u to the profit share π. Dynamics are presented explicitly in Figure 5.3.

The other side of Marx-Goodwin macroeconomic adjustment is a positive effect of π on u, assuming that demand is in practice profit-led. It is illustrated by the "Demand" curve in Figure 5.1. Initially, medium-run macro equilibrium is at point F, with π and u following clockwise cycles around it (see Figure 5.3).

The diagram provides a plausible explanation for the trends post-1980 mentioned in Chapter 3 – rising u and π, falling or stable ω. For reasons already discussed, the $\pi(u)$ schedule drifted upward over the past thirty or forty years. This pattern shows up in Figure 3.1. The labor share $\psi = 1 - \pi$, and $\psi = \omega/\xi$ with $\xi = X/L$ as labor productivity. Because of shifts in labor market institutions, ω has been stable while ξ has increased relatively over time, shifting the functional income distribution toward profits and stimulating demand. The demand push shifted the focal point of the economy from point F to G.

The adverse effect on demand from lagging low incomes can make the $u(\pi)$ curve in Figure 5.1 steep – a large increase in π is needed to boost u The squeeze on the middle class due to rising profits (and transfers to the bottom 60 percent) illustrated in Figures 2.3 and 2.4 has been instrumental in supporting the post-1980 upward trend in capital utilization shown in Figure 3.1.

MAINSTREAM DYNAMICS OF CAPITAL

The medium run is all well and good, but what happens over longer stretches of time? The theory of economic growth attempts to answer this question. It focuses on a "steady state" as a description of the "long run" in which all relevant variables are increasing at the same exponential rate, say capital stock growth $g-\delta$ with $g = I/K$ and δ as the depreciation rate.

As discussed in Chapter 3, mainstream growth theory presumes that macroeconomic performance is determined from the side of supply. Since it underlies so much discussion it makes sense to give a quick sketch. The basic assumptions have already been laid out in Chapter 3.

The Solow-Swan version of the model assumes that there is a constant saving rate from both capital and labor incomes. More "classical" specifications are based on the Cambridge polymath Frank Ramsey's (1928) model of "optimal" saving over time. The analysis is set up in terms of the ratio of capital to "effective" labor λ (i.e., the fully employed labor force times a factor representing productivity which grows exogenously over time). Call the capital/effective labor ratio k. Capital is the economy's only asset and source of wealth. On neoclassical assumptions, it is subject to decreasing returns and the profit rate is supposed to equal capital's marginal product.

Suppose that initially there is a high level of k as in the USA post-1980. If there is a lot of plant and equipment sitting around, profitability will be low. In a perfectly foreseen future, k will fall and the profit rate will be higher. In anticipation, the asset price of capital (call it q) should rise.

"Society's" marginal utility of consumption, whatever that means for a class-ridden collection of diverse households, is supposed to equal q. (The more common assumption is that households equate marginal utility to the price of consumer goods; q enters here because a saving versus consumption choice is involved.) The higher the level of consumption, the lower marginal utility will be. Low q is associated with high consumption per head. At any time, growth accounting states that

Change in k = Output/λ − consumption/λ − $n \times k$.

Capital per unit of effective labor will increase if output rises. It will fall if consumption per labor goes up. It also decreases in proportion to a "natural" growth rate n equaling the sum of growth rates of population and productivity which both reduce capital stock per unit of effective labor.

If consumption is initially high, the change in k will be negative. Consumption should then fall over time because, spurred by the low profit rate, q rises. The upshot is that growth rate of k becomes less negative. Eventually the economy reaches a steady state with a constant q and capital growing at the natural rate.

In the Solow-Swan model, k goes down from an initially high level simply because with decreasing returns to capital, saving falls short of the level needed to support growth at the natural rate. A *lower* level of k will *increase* the output/λ ratio, push up saving, and steer the system toward steady state growth at the natural rate. All that optimal growth theory does is graft fanciful teleological asset price and saving dynamics onto Solow-Swan.[4]

Almost all mainstream models such as the one by Eggertsson et al. (2018) cited previously adopt the optimal growth specification. Since it is so manifestly unrealistic one has to wonder why they bother.

---

[4] Additional assumptions are extreme. All households have the same income profile and tastes regarding present and future consumption. They have perfect foresight over future asset prices forever. Only one initial value of q will be consistent with convergence to a steady state. Solow-Swan and Say's Law are tame by comparison.

MORE PLAUSIBLE GROWTH DYNAMICS

The assumptions adopted herein are radically different from the mainstream's: (i) labor is not fully employed, with the level of employment responding to output and labor productivity while capital sets the scale of the macro economy; (ii) output is determined by effective demand and adjusts to make total saving equal investment which follows from independent relationships; (iii) as discussed, the distribution of income (= output) between profits and wages is determined by conflict between capital and labor under institutions which may change over time; and (iv) saving rates from wages and profits differ. These assumptions fit well with recent US macroeconomic history.

A further issue is that, in practice, business undertakes most private investment and saving. The convention in growth theory is that all capital is owned directly by households – income of households and business is consolidated into a single private sector. Capital, as noted above, is the only asset, implicitly estimated by perpetual inventory methods. The whole structure of financial claims illustrated in Figure 3.7 for the US distribution of wealth is whisked away. In the modeling here, there is still an independent investment function and a distinction between "capitalist" and "worker" households who save. In the simplest versions, capitalists own a share Z of total wealth (i.e., capital) and receive no wages (Pasinetti, 1962 and 1974).

If capitalists hold capital K_c let $Z = K_c/K$. The respective saving rates of the two classes are s_c and s_w, with $s_c > s_w$. Capitalists receive profits rK_c on the capital they own, while workers get the rest of income. Figures 2.3 and 2.4 show that capital gains are crucial in practice; they are a key transfer vehicle of profits toward rich households. As discussed in previous chapters, the top 1 percent can, to a good approximation, be seen as capitalists.

Figure 5.2 shows how the model may arrive at a steady state. The growth rate $\hat{Z}$ of Z is the difference between the rates of K_c and K ($\hat{K}_c$ and $\hat{K}$ respectively). Capitalists' income and saving increase with the

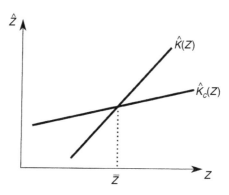

FIGURE 5.2 Dynamics of the capitalists' wealth share Z around a Pasinetti steady state at $\overline{Z}$

profit rate so $\hat{K}_c$ rises with r. But then the question is, how does r depend on Z? Because s_c is relatively high, an increase in Z will raise saving overall and reduce aggregate demand. The demand curve in Figure 5.1 will shift downward (to the left), raising $\pi = r/u$ and reducing u. With higher r and π, $\hat{K}_c$ in Figure 5.2 becomes an increasing function of Z.

As discussed in connection with equation (5A.3) in the Appendix, available saving increases with both π and u, so that $\hat{K}$ is an increasing function of Z as well. If a positive response of $\hat{K}$ to Z is strong enough there will be a stable steady state at $\overline{Z}$ in Figure 5.2.[5] The growth rate at $\overline{Z}$ is determined by interactions of saving by capitalists and the total. It does not have to be equal to some natural rate.

As already noted, steady growth means that all relevant variables increase at the same exponential rate $g–\delta$. For all variables, the ratios of their increases over time to their levels must be the same.

Two useful formulas follow. One is Pasinetti's elegant relationship

---

[5] That is, $\hat{Z} = \hat{K}_c - \hat{K}$. If the positive effect of Z on $\hat{K}$ is stronger than on $\hat{K}_c$, then in Figure 5.2 there is a steeper schedule for $\hat{K}$ than for $\hat{K}_c$. The wealth share Z rises when $\hat{K} < \hat{K}_c$. For details about convergence see the Appendix to this chapter and Taylor et al. (2019).

$$s_c r = g \qquad\qquad (5.1)$$

which shows that the capitalists' (gross) saving rate mediates the magnitudes of the investment/capital ratio and profit rate. With $s_c < 1$ we already have $r > g$, an inequality which Piketty (2014) emphasizes. It is a corollary of steady state accounting, not some newly discovered law of capitalism.

Second, the steady state flow/stock condition just mentioned implies that workers' share of wealth is

$$1 - Z = [s_w/(s_c - s_w)][(1 - \pi)/\pi]. \qquad\qquad (5.2)$$

Wealth shares are intimately related to the distribution of income between profits and wages, and thereby social change and redistributive policy. The driving parameters are savings rates and the steady state profit share. Because the capital stock growth rate is fixed, investment behavior does not figure in the determination of Z at steady state.[6] In practice, the steady state will not be reached in finite time, but along with Pasinetti's relationship (5.1), equation (5.2) will apply approximately if the economy is nearby.

The workers' share, $1 - Z$, increases with s_w and decreases with s_c and π. The former effect reflects Meade's (1964) observation that wages are a potential source of saving unavailable to rentiers, setting an upper limit to Z. Because of their different sources of income, both classes coexist in steady state.

Even so, the upper bound may be high. On the back of another envelope, a plausible saving rate for the top 1 percent of households is in the vicinity of $s_c = 0.5$. The rate for the rest (middle class with positive saving and poorer households with negative) could be $s_w = 0.1$. The corporate profit share of GDP is in the range of 0.25. In the household accounts, the combined GDP share of proprietors' incomes, rent, and depreciation is about 0.12; so, the overall return to capital might be around 0.33. These numbers generate a steady state

---

[6]   Away from the steady state Z will be evolving as in equation (5A.6) in the Appendix, influenced by both investment and saving. See Taylor et al. (2019).

value for Z of 0.5, above the level of 0.4 for the top 1 percent of wealth-holders shown in Figure 3.6 and shared by most authors today.[7]

CYCLICAL DISTRIBUTION AND DEMAND DYNAMICS

The great historian (and jazz critic) Eric Hobsbawm (1994) talked about rhythms of economic life, not oscillations or cycles. Economists, lacking Hobsbawm's depth of insight, have seized upon simple (-minded) dynamical models to try to summarize movements in economic variables. They may help a bit, as a formal representation of medium-term distribution versus demand illustrates.

Figure 5.3 is a revised version of Figure 5.1. It is a *phase diagram, a* picture invented by physicists and mathematicians in the late nineteenth century (economists are always playing catch-up with the tricks of the trade in higher powered disciplines). The diagrams are used to illustrate trajectories over time of two variables – u and π in the present instance – determined by a pair of ordinary differential equations. The equations describe how the variables evolve, beginning at some initial (u,π) point.

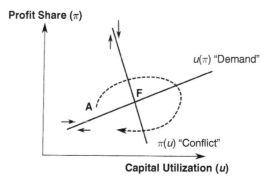

FIGURE 5.3 Cyclical dynamics of the profit share π and capital utilization u

---

[7] Ederer and Rehm (2020) get similar results for European countries except when workers' saving rates are very low. In Chapter 6's simulations, the wealth share of the top 1 percent approaches 60 percent.

The schedules introduced in Figure 5.1 now represent *null-clines* along which one or the other variable is stable (with "null" motion). For example the $u(\pi)$ nullcline shows combinations of the levels of two variables – u and π – for which u is constant (i.e., $du/dt = \dot{u} = f(u,\pi) = 0$). The small horizontal arrows show how u moves when it does not lie on the nullcline. The arrows pointing toward the nullcline show that adjustment of u is *stable*. That is, for a given level of π, if u lies below (to the left of) the value along the nullcline, then it tends to rise. The small vertical arrows signal stable adjustment of π toward the $\pi(u)$ nullcline for a given value of u. The slopes of the nullclines suggest that demand responds positively to π while the profit share responds negatively to u.

As in Figure 5.1, F is a focal point for the system: the variables spiral around it. For a trajectory beginning at point A, for example, the small arrows show that both u and π should rise until they cross the nullcline for π. Then π starts to fall and π continues to rise until the path crosses the nullcline for u, after which both variables decline. As discussed, such a trajectory is a fair representation of US cyclical dynamics following World War II. For a proper description of the institutions and history, you must rely on somebody like Hobsbawm.

VALUATION RATIO AND INTEREST RATE

Let's go back to treating capital's asset price as the valuation ratio $q = P_e E/PK$. Figure 3.5 suggests it has a degree of cyclicality, with an upswing since the 1970s. This observation runs counter to the monotonic q dynamics built into optimal saving models.

Along the lines of Chapter 3, cyclicality of q can be contrasted with "the" real financial interest rate j. It was stable or declining until the mid-1970s, shot up for a decade during the anti-inflationary "Volcker shock." Then, until early 2017, the interest rate trended downward, in part due to falling inflation due to nominal wage repression and successive Greenspan-Bernanke-Yellen-Powell "puts," mentioned in Chapter 3.

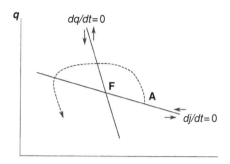

FIGURE 5.4 Dynamics of the valuation ratio q and the real interest rate j

Nobody can reliably analyze the stock market, but it is fair to ask if these movements are somehow related, especially in view of Piketty's emphasis on the significance of asset price changes for the distribution of wealth. The phase diagram of a simple model is shown in Figure 5.4, with details in the Appendix.

In standard theory, asset prices such as P_e are subject to positive feedback, that is, the time derivative $\dot{P}_e$ is positively related to the price level P_e. The usual story is that capital gains $\dot{P}_e E$ contribute to the return $\rho P_e E$ to holding equity (with ρ as the "relevant" rate of return). The *change* $\dot{P}_e$ in the asset price can of course only be observed ex post (after the current moment), but an assumption of "perfect myopic foresight" takes care of such a minor objection.

Positive feedback carries over to q. Meanwhile a low value of the real interest rate is likely to be associated with a high q. The nullcline for $\dot{q} = dq/dt = 0$ takes the configuration shown in Figure 5.4. Positive feedback means that $\dot{q}$ rises when for a given j, q lies above the nullcline (small arrows).

Dynamics of q can be stabilized by the interest rate. A low rate is supposed to stimulate investment, so $\partial g/\partial j < 0$, making $\dot{q}$ an increasing function of j. Because $\dot{q}$ responds positively to both q and j, the variables trade off inversely to hold it constant in Figure 5.4. The negative slope of the nullcline for dq/dt captures the positive effects. If one variable rises, the other must fall to hold $dq/dt = 0$.

Because of capitalization, a low value of j is likely to be associated with high q and $\dot{q}$. A low value of q will shift portfolios away from equity, bidding up j. If there is stable adjustment of j around a nullcline with $dj/dt = 0$, we get a negative slope in Figure 5.4.

There is a steady state at point F in this two-dimensional system. If the initial condition at A involves a relatively high interest rate and low valuation ratio, j would begin to fall and q to rise. After a time (perhaps a decade or three) the trajectory would cross the nullcline for $dq/dt = 0$, and q would begin to fall. There would be overshooting in the sense that j would continue to fall for a time, but ultimately would reverse course.

The model is simplistic, but it does underline a key point visible in Figure 3.5. There is no reason to expect an asset price such as q to retain its level or trend indefinitely. Positive feedback inevitably destabilizes a dynamical system.

MACROECONOMIC FORCES

These models suggest three important points about macroeconomic behavior, two regarding the role of financial markets and the last about performance of the economy's real side over time.

Macro orthodoxy as of 2019 centers on the idea that short- to medium-run performance is determined by "loanable funds," already mentioned. Examples include the visibly nonexistent "zero lower bound" on interest rates, which is allegedly holding down investment, the global "savings glut" keeping the interest rate near zero, and the "dynamic stochastic general equilibrium" (DSGE) models like the mainstream narrative discussed previously.

The loanable funds idea dates back to the early nineteenth century and was restated forcefully by the Swedish economist Knut Wicksell around the turn of the twentieth. It was repudiated in 1936 by Keynes in his *General Theory* (before that he was merely an important post-Wicksellian rather than the greatest economist of his and later times). Like Keynes, Wicksell recognized that saving and investment have different determining factors and also thought that households provide most saving. He argued that the interest rate will adjust to assure macro balance. If saving falls short of investment, then the real interest rate j will increase. Households will save more and firms invest less. The supply of loanable funds will go up and demand will go down until the two flows equalize.

One problem, as we have seen, is that households are not the dominant source of private saving. Business firms are, and their saving is a residual. If the interest rate rises, then their outgoing financial transfers could go up, forcing saving down. Second, the evidence in favor of interest rate effects on household saving and business investment is weak. Residential investment does respond to j but is a small share of the total. In light of the data, the theory simply does not work. This conclusion is only strengthened by the fact that government and the rest of the world are major sources of (respectively negative and positive) saving which may in fact vary inversely with the interest rate (Taylor, 2017).

Loanable funds is a *flow* theory of the interest rate. Keynes replaced it with models in which markets for *stocks* of assets determine their prices and rates of return. The discussion here of q versus j is one example. It suggests that joint movements of these two financial variables play the key role in setting their levels over time.

The second important point is that the interest rate is often assigned a key role in shaping the business cycle (a tradition dating to well before Keynes's discussion of the "trade cycle" in *General Theory*). The gist can be summarized in terms of a diagram similar to Figure 5.3. The initial increase in π would be mirrored by a fall in the wage share, which would subsequently move upward and choke off demand. The interest rate and (as discussed) the yield premium follow a similar path.

In practice, Rezai (2013) argues that only households increase their investment minus saving (or net borrowing) when the interest rate is lowered. As just noted, business and government saving may well increase as a lower j reduces their debt service obligations. In other words, household net borrowing leads the demand cycle while business and government lag. When interest rate effects are brought into the econometrics, the distributive cycle in Figure 5.3 persists, only marginally affected by movements in the interest rate.

The final topic is how wage repression can lead to secular stagnation. The shifts in the structure of production noted in Chapter 4 are a contributing factor. Redistribution toward profits, moreover, can hold down aggregate demand in the short to medium run, especially if it harms low-income earners with negative rates of saving. Demand may also be held down by unbalanced finance, which raises capital gains flowing toward high-saving rich households. Induced innovation arguments as in Chapter 4 suggest that a falling wage, especially if it is engineered by labor repression, will hold down the rate of productivity growth.

Distribution and demand can interact in a vicious circle. The question is whether it is possible to introduce virtue into the loop.

APPENDIX: EINIGE KLEINE ALGEBRA

With apologies to Mozart and those who don't like low-level math, sketches of the equations underlying the charts in this chapter appear here.

LOW INCOME–LED DEMAND?

Before getting into high and low labor incomes, let π and ψ respectively stand for the shares of profits and all wages in income. Evidently,

$$\pi + \psi = 1 \tag{5A.1}$$

Let s_π and s_ψ be saving rates from these income flows, with $s_\pi > s_\psi$. Saving per unit of capital, say σ, becomes

$$\sigma = (s_\pi \pi + s_\psi \psi)u = [(s_\pi - s_\psi)\pi + s_\psi]u \tag{5A.2}$$

in which u is the output/capital ratio. The expression to the far right follows from (5A.1).

Suppose that investment demand is

$$g = I/K = g_0 + \alpha_r r + \alpha_u u = g_0 + (\alpha_r \pi + \alpha_u)u. \tag{5A.3}$$

The α_r coefficient captures the stimulus from the profit rate r to g, and α_u represents an accelerator. The term to the right follows from the relationship $r = \pi u$ discussed in previous chapters. Macro balance in a demand-determined system dictates that

$$g - \sigma = 0.$$

This equation solves to give

$$u = g_0/\Delta \tag{5A.4}$$

with

$$\Delta = [(s_\pi - s_\psi) - \alpha_r]\pi + s_\psi - \alpha_u \tag{5A.5}$$

as the inverse of the multiplier $1/\Delta$ in (5A.4).

If $\alpha_r > (s_\pi - s_\psi)$ y, then an increase in π will reduce Δ and raise u. This is the gist of profit-led demand. The inequality basically says that in an economy closed to trade, if investment responds more strongly than saving to profits, then demand will be profit-led (effects via exports in an open economy might strengthen this result). One can also show that investment $g = I/K$ will increase with π if

$$\alpha_r s_\psi - \alpha_u(s_\pi - s_\psi) = (\alpha_r + \alpha_u)s_\psi - \alpha_u s_\pi > 0$$

(i.e., $s_\psi > 0$, the accelerator is not strong, and the saving rate differential is small). A higher capital stock growth rate will spill over to output expansion as well.

These results require a cozy little two-class macroeconomy, closed to foreign trade. Suppose, however, that there are "poor" and "middle class" wage earners with respective shares ψ_p and ψ_m in total income, and saving rates s_p and s_m. The numbers in previous chapters suggest that $s_m > s_p$ and quite possibly $s_p < 0$.

With these modifications, (5A.1) becomes

$$\pi + \psi_p + \psi_m = 1 \tag{5A.1'}$$

so that an increase in π must be met by a reduction in ψ_p or ψ_m. Saving per unit of capital becomes

$$\sigma = (s_\pi \pi + s_p \psi_p + s_m \psi_m)u. \tag{5A.2'}$$

The inverse multiplier now is

$$\Delta = (s_\pi - \alpha_r)\pi + s_p \psi_p + s_m \psi_m - \alpha_u. \tag{5A.5'}$$

It is argued in a two-class context that steady capital stock growth can occur if (in present notation) $\alpha_r > s_\pi$. We can consider an increase in the profit share matched by an equal reduction in the low income wage share ψ_p while ψ_m stays constant so that (5A.1') is satisfied. Then

$$d\Delta/d\pi = (s_\pi - \alpha_r) - s_p$$

If s_p is negative then $d\Delta/d\pi > 0$ when $-s_p > \alpha_r - s_\pi$. That is, the low-income group's consumption loss from a lower income share ψ_p due to a jump in π outweighs higher investment minus the saving leakage coming from higher profits. The multiplier $1/\Delta$ falls so the rise in profits is contractionary. Demand is strongly low-income led.

WEALTH DYNAMICS

For any variable x, recall that $\dot{x} = dx/dt$ and $\hat{x} = \dot{x}/x$. In the Pasinetti worker vs. capitalist growth model described in the text, expansion of capitalists' capital is determined by their saving,

$$\hat{K}_c = s_c r - \delta = s_c \pi u - \delta$$

since (from Chapter 2) $r = \pi u$.

From total saving, growth of capital is given by

$$\hat{K} = \sigma - \delta = (s_c - s_w)rZ \\ + s_w u - \delta = [(s_c - s_w)\pi Z + s_w]u - \delta$$

We can ignore u in both equations. As a function of Z, the slope of the $\hat{K}_c(Z)$ schedule in Figure 5.2 is determined by $s_c \pi_Z$. The $\hat{K}(Z)$ schedule's slope will be driven by $(s_c - s_w)(\pi + Z\pi_Z)$. If $\pi_Z > 0$ is "small," then the $\hat{K}(Z)$ schedule will be less steep than $\hat{K}_c(Z)$, and the Pasinetti equilibrium will be stable. Instability can arise with a "large" value of π_Z. Then an increase in Z will increase the slope of

$\hat{K}_c(Z)$ relative to $\hat{K}(Z)$. If $\hat{K}_c(Z)$ becomes steeper than $\hat{K}(Z)$ in Figure 5.2, the model will diverge.

In more formal terms, the differential equation for Z can be written as[8]

$$\dot{Z} = Z\{[s_c(1 - Z) + s_w Z]\pi - s_w\}u \qquad (5A.6)$$

The "official" stability condition is $d\dot{Z}/dZ < 0$ at the steady state. It will be satisfied for a small value of π_Z. The steady state level of Z is given by equation (5.2).

Valuation Ratio and Interest Rate

An example of positive feedback in the asset price P_e is the well-known business school Gordon (1959) equation for valuing a firm's share price. It captures the point emphasized in previous chapters about how capital gains are an important vehicle for transferring profits to households. The formula is

$$\rho P_e E = \dot{P}_e E + \theta PK. \qquad (5A.7)$$

The coefficient ρ is the market's "required" return to equity, famously in the range of 7 percent (or 0.07) in the USA. There are two components to the return. One is dividends scaled to capital, θPK. The other is capital gains or $\dot{P}_e E$ with E as an index of equity outstanding.

One can rewrite (5A.7) to show the positive feedback more clearly,

$$\dot{P}_e = P_e[\rho - (\theta/q)]$$

with $q = P_e E/PK$. The change in E over time is

$$P_e \dot{E} = \chi PK.$$

For the last few decades, χ has been negative because of share buybacks. The growth of the capital stock is $\hat{K} = g - \delta$, and we can assume that its price P is constant.

---

[8]   Dutt (1990) and Palley (2012) earlier stressed the significance of dynamics of Z in the analysis of wealth.

Combining all these equations gives the change in q over time,

$$\dot{q} = q(\rho - g + \delta) + \chi - \theta, \tag{5A.8}$$

in which buybacks (with $\chi < 0$) and dividends both reduce $\dot{q}$ but raise q at a steady state described by the equation

$$q = (\theta - \chi)/(\rho - g + \delta). \tag{5A.9}$$

Because ρ will exceed g-δ, q would be positive at the steady state

What about the stability? Differentiating (5A.8) with respect to q and plugging in (5A.9) gives

$$d\dot{q}/dq = [(\theta - \chi)/q] - q(\partial g/\partial q). \tag{5A.10}$$

Presumably, a higher q stimulates investment demand, so $\partial g/\partial q > 0$. But unless this effect is strong, it will be true that $d\dot{q}/dq > 0$, and (5A.8) will be unstable. Figure 5.4 shows how it can be cyclically stabilized by dynamics of the interest rate.

6   Possible Future Prospects

(coauthor Özlem Ömer)

Illustrating how the three income classes may fare under various circumstances is the goal of simulations from a demand-driven model of economic growth discussed in this chapter. It uses the SAM of Figure 2.2 as the database. The model's key assumptions draw on ideas previously discussed. A succinct list follows.

MODELING POSSIBLE PROSPECTS

In the short to medium run, total supply (GDP + imports) is determined by effective demand, which is influenced by the income distribution. Consumption and business investment depend directly on distribution. Along with imports and some taxes, they also increase with output. Reflecting the fact that the major financial transfers are between business and households, payments of interest and dividends are proportional to profits. To maintain a medium-term perspective, other fiscal variables (including government spending and transfers to households) and exports are scaled to the capital stock as a metric for the size of the economic system.

There can be a medium run profit squeeze. The growth rate of the wage share $(\hat{\psi})$ is determined as the difference between real wage and productivity growth rates $(\hat{\omega}$ and $\hat{\xi}$ respectively), $\hat{\psi} = \hat{\omega} - \hat{\xi}$. Growth of the profit share $(\hat{\pi})$ follows from macro-cost accounting $(\psi + \pi = 1)$. In the results below, $\hat{\omega}$ and $\hat{\xi}$ are controlled as parameters, although the model could be extended to permit them to be determined endogenously.[1] Productivity growth is set at 1.4 percent per year, while different levels of $\hat{\omega}$ are considered.[2]

Year-on-year, the short-run solution is determined by effective demand and distribution. To get numerical results, all the flows in Figure 2.2 have to be tracked; the accounting is straightforward but the details are a mess.

SHORT-TERM POLICY PERSPECTIVES

The model at hand creates numbers to fill in a SAM and WAM, subject to their static and dynamic accounting restrictions. The focus is on thought experiments regarding plausible macroeconomic perspectives. Such exercises can be useful, but have their limitations. The best possible SAM-based model for, say, China in 1980 would have projected a poor, stagnant economy. Unless its designer were a productivity and effective demand oracle, the model would not have revealed the cumulative growth process that was about to unfold.

A first step in understanding a model is to explore how it rearranges the base-year SAM in response to exogenous shifts in levels of variables or parameters ("comparative statics" in the jargon). To get some feel for magnitudes, look at the tax reductions in 2017 and 2018. Their size is on the order of 1 trillion dollars *over ten years*. The implied perturbation of 100 billion dollars per year in a 20 trillion dollar economy is around half a percent of GDP. In terms of 2019 macroeconomics, $100 billion is *not* a large number, nor is it gigantic in political terms.

For example, a very low-end estimate of the scale of interventions needed to mitigate global warming is 2 percent of GDP (Rezai et al. 2018). If, in the USA, that took the form of higher government

---

[1]   For simplicity, we did not deal with nominal wage and price inflation rates as illustrated in Figure I.2. The model could readily be extended to bring them into the picture. The implicit assumption is that (across business cycles) inflation does not have strong effects on the real economy.

[2]   The 1.4 percent rate reflects historical trends. As illustrated in Figure I.1, productivity growth tailed off after 2010, so we make an implicit assumption that it will recover. In any case, in the model's balanced growth runs, as will be discussed, $\hat{\xi}$ basically serves as a benchmark.

spending, then the 2019 level of G would rise by some $400 billion. Medicare is basically a fiscal transfer program. Free college tuition could be another. If enhanced Medicare brings 20 million people into the health care system at $15,000 each, the cost would be about $300 billion. Reduced tuition might cost roughly the same. We have a grand total of a trillion dollars per year, or 5 percent of GDP. By way of comparison, US defense spending is a bit over 3 percent. According to the International Monetary Fund, energy subsidies are twice as high.

Figures 6.1 and 6.2 summarize macroeconomic and distributive effects of a few more modest changes.

In row B of Figure 6.1, an increase of government current spending (or "G") of $100 billion raises GDP by $158 billion and the fiscal deficit by $58 billion. The implied multipliers of 1.58 and 0.58 are in the usually accepted ranges. Effects on distribution in Figure 6.2 are

	Macroeconomic Impacts of Policy Shifts (Level vs % Change)		
POLICY	Real GDP (Trillions)	Government Deficit(−Sg) (Trillions)	Current Account(Sr) (Trillions)
A	Initial Level	17.350	0.285	0.405
B	Increase Gov. spending by 0.1 trillion	0.154, (0.88 %)	0.058, (20.3 %)	0.025, (6.3%)
C	Increase Gov. spending by 0.25 trillion, tax middle class by 0.1 trillion and top 1% by 0.15	0.145, (0.83 %)	−0.041, (−14.5 %)	0.024, (5.9 %)
D	Increase Taxes by 0.05 trillion for top 2 classes, transfer it to bottom 60% of HH	0.08, (0.46 %)	−0.023, (−8.3 %)	0.013, (3.2 %)
E	Increase bottom 60% of HH wages by 10%	0.227, (1.30 %)	−0.041, (−14.5 %)	0.037, (9.3 %)

FIGURE 6.1 Macroeconomic impacts of policy shifts (level changes and percentage changes)

Level Changes in Distribution from Policy Shift (Level vs % Change)

	POLICY	Bottom 60% Mean Disposable Income (thousands)	Bottom 60% Size (millions)	61–99 % Mean Disposable Income (thousands)	61-99 % Size (millions)	Top 1 % Mean Disposable Income (thousands)	Top 1% Size (million)	Palma (Top1% Mean Income/Bottom 60% Mean Income)	Palma (Top1% Mean Disposable Income/Bottom 60% Mean Disposable Income)	Palma (Top1% Mean Income/61-99% Mean Income)	Palma (Top1 % Mean Disposable Income/61–99% Mean Disposable Income)
A	Initial Level	55.48	74.9	138.5	47	1765.9	1.2	39.06	31.82	13.3	12.74
B	Increase Gov. spending by 0.1 trillion	-0.224, (-0.4 %)	0.66, (0.88 %)	-0.084, (-0.06 %)	0.41, (0.88 %)	-0.088, (-0.005 %)	0.01, (0.88 %)	0.14, (0.36 %)	0.12, (0.4 %)	0.006, (0.05 %)	0.007, (0.05 %)
C	Increase Gov. spending by 0.25 trillion, tax middle class by 0.1 trillion and top 1% by 0.15	-0.211, (-0.38 %)	0.62, (0.83 %)	-2.20, (-1.59 %)	0.39, (0.83 %)	-125, (-7 %)	0.01, (0.83 %)	0.13, (0.34 %)	-2.14, (-6.7 %)	0.006, (0.04 %)	-0.71, (-5.5 %)
D	Increase Taxes by 0.05 trillion for top 2 classes, transfer it to bottom 60% of HH	1.192, (2.14 %)	0.34, (0.46 %)	-1.10, (-0.79 %)	0.21, (0.46 %)	-41.7, (-2.36 %)	0.005, (0.46 %)	-0.74, (-1.9 %)	-1.4, (-4.4 %)	0.003, (0.02 %)	-0.2, (-1.5 %)
E	Increase bottom 60% of HH wages by 10%	1.921, (-1.446 %)	0.98, (1.3 %)	-1.01, (-0.72 %)	0.61, (1.3 %)	-28.9, (-1.6 %)	0.015, (1.3 %)	-2, (25.2 %)	-1.5, (-4.9 %)	-0.12, (-0.94 %)	-0.11, (-0.9 %)

FIGURE 6.2 Distributional impacts of policy changes

minimal. Similarly to output, numbers of employed households go up by 0.88 percent.

Row C in Figure 6.1 shows the effects of a larger "balanced budget" (initially) expansion, with $250 billion of extra spending offset by tax increases of $100 and $150 billion for the upper two income groups (by roughly 10 percent for the middle class and 20 percent for the rich respectively, close to the top of "politically acceptable" levels?).[3] The fiscal deficit falls and GDP increases with a multiplier of 0.58. In Figure 6.2, due to higher taxes, the after-tax Palma ratio for the top to bottom group goes down by 6.7 percent, a minimal shift in comparison to the trends shown in Figure 1.2.

Row D in Figure 6.1 shows the macro impacts of raising taxes by $50 billion each for the two upper groups and transferring the proceeds to the bottom 60 percent of households, increasing their pretax income by 2 percent. In line with the discussion in Chapters 2 and 5 of negative saving at the bottom, this $100 billion "balanced budget" tax/transfer package is expansionary. It increases GDP by $80 billion, and reduces the fiscal deficit. In Figure 6.2, mean disposable income per poor household rises by more than 2 percent. The top-to-bottom Palma ratio for disposable income goes down by 4.4 percent, although it remains very high. These results suggest that short-run redistributive policy can be effective but will fall far short of reversing fifty years of increasing income inequality.

A similar observation applies to 10 percent real wage hikes at the bottom, broadly in line with the minimum wage increases analyzed by the Congressional Budget Office (2014). Again reflecting the negative saving rates of households in the bottom 60 percent, Row E in Figure 6.1 shows that output is low income–led – higher wages are expansionary with a magnitude similar to the tax/transfer package. The same observation applies to the distributive indicators in Figure 6.2.[4]

---

[3]   Recall from Chapter 1 that direct plus indirect tax rates for both groups are around 22 percent. Hence households in the one percent would pay an average rate of about 26.5 percent and the middle class would face 24 percent.

[4]   Minimum wage increases in the 25 percent range were under discussion in 2018–19. The expansionary effect would be scaled up accordingly.

It is worth noting, however, that the benefits of redistribution may be overstated for several reasons. The US transfer system effectively "taxes" income increases at the bottom of the size distribution by reducing benefits when extra money comes in. A rough estimate of the tax rate is 30 percent (CBO, 2014). As hinted in previous chapters, firms may cut back on employment (or raise labor productivity) in response to higher labor costs.

The bottom line is that short-run policy initiatives within ranges typically discussed will not strongly affect distribution in the US economy. Such results are built into the accounting structure of any macro model based on a SAM. See Gale et al. (2015) and Taylor et al. (2017, written in 2014) for similar findings.

Modifying taxes and transfers within the 10 percent of output that could readily be manipulated by the government or increasing wages at the bottom by 10 percent (or even 25 percent) simply cannot offset the big shift of GDP toward the top income group that occurred after the 1970s. Cumulating changes would be required. We can use the model to explore possibilities.

REAL WAGES, PRODUCTIVITY, AND GROWTH

The model's performance over time obeys distributive dynamics based on differential equations for growth of the capital stock and accumulation of wealth. They follow from accounting and a few key assumptions outlined below.

Simulations over a few decades at most will have relevance to current debates. Before going into the details, it makes sense to ask how the model behaves over the very long run. Figure 6.3 suggests that solutions do stabilize over a span of 100 years. Three variants are considered: "balanced growth" with both productivity and the real wage rising at 1.4 percent per year (thereby holding the profit share constant) and runs in which the wage grows at 1.3 percent and at 1.5 percent.

Levels and growth rates of both capital and GDP are set from the demand side. The ratio of gross business investment to capital

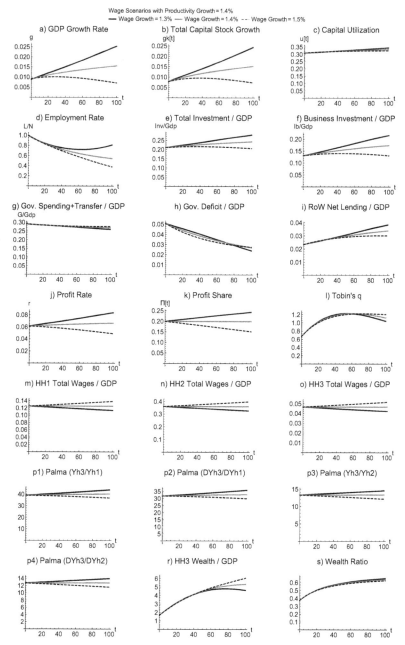

FIGURE 6.3 Wage Scenarios with 1.4 percent productivity growth

responds to the profit rate with a coefficient (α_r in Chapter 5) of 0.7, making overall investment slightly more sensitive than saving to r.[5] As a consequence, capital utilization is higher at the lower growth rate of the real wage; effective demand is very weakly profit-led (panel c in the diagram). GDP and capital growth rates are much more sensitive to changes in profits (panels a and b), but visible divergences in growth rates appear only after two or three decades.

A steady state is possible only along the balanced growth trajectory, with both $\hat{K}$ and $\hat{X}$ tending toward 1.5 percent per year. Consistent with Pasinetti, this growth rate lies well below the rate of profit (the implied value of $\hat{X}$, if equation (5.1) were to apply literally to a model as complex as the one at hand, is around 0.25). Growth rates are higher (lower) with slower (faster) wage increases. Similar patterns are observed for investment (panels e and f) and employment (panel d).

The charts toward the bottom of the figure illustrate distributive shifts. Panels m, n, and o show changing GDP shares of wage payments that move in opposite directions to changes in profits. Palma ratios for total and disposable incomes of the top households with respect to the other two fall consistently with faster wage growth. Over time, shifts in the functional income distribution influence the positions of households. But they need years to take effect. The wealth share of the top 1 percent ("HH3") trends toward 60 percent or slightly higher.

Figure 6.4 presents cumulative effects of differential real wage and productivity growth rates over a four-decade "medium run." Results from wage growth rates of 1.15 percent, 1.4 percent (balanced growth), and 1.75 percent are shown. Over a similar period in the past, Figure I.1 shows that profits began to trend upward around 1970, while Figure 1.3 illustrates how labor income lagged output per household. The strongly trending Palma ratios in Figure 1.2 were the result.

In panels j and k, there are visible shifts in the profit rate and share. In a profit-led model, they affect growth rates in panels a and b.

---

[5]   This is basically the stability condition illustrated in Figure 5.2. The parameter value of 0.7 is consistent with estimates by Storm and Naastepad, 2012.

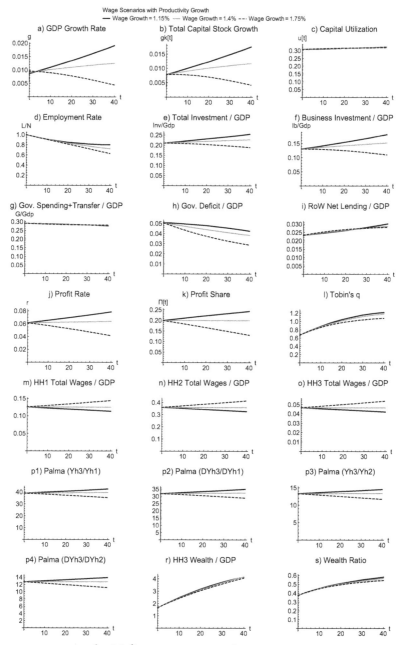

FIGURE 6.4 Medium run wage scenarios

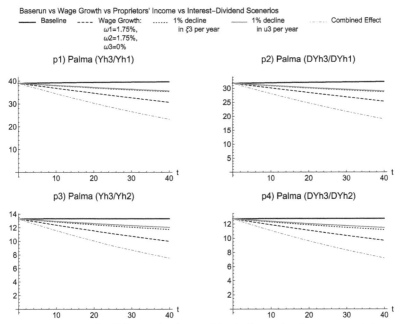

FIGURE 6.5 Palma ratios for combined effects of real wage growth for
nonrich households and downward trends in financial and proprietors'
incomes for the top 1 percent

In panels m through o, wages of course move in opposite directions to
profits, and faster wage growth (dashed lines) cuts back on the Palma
ratios.

As emphasized in Chapter 1, rising income for the top 1 percent
was driven by increases in wages, proprietors' receipts, and financial
transfers. Figure 6.5 shows Palma ratios over time for model simulations under four assumptions: (i) 1.75 percent real wage growth
for the bottom two household groups and zero growth for the top;
(ii) a 1 percent annual decrease in the coefficient tying rich proprietors'
incomes to output; (iii) 1 percent annual decrease in the coefficient
relating financial transfers to the upper 1 percent to profits; (iv) all of
the above. These numbers are of course arbitrary, but illustrative. The
balanced growth solution is a baseline. Individual effects of (i) – (iii),
which reduce the Palmas, are shown, along with the combined result

(iv). Faster real wage growth (i) by itself has a larger effect on the Palmas than the other two (both are about equal). Over four decades, differential growth rates can cumulate visibly.

With all effects combined, the Palma ratios slide down toward the levels of the mid-1980s shown in Figure 1.2. But, as in the past, it would take decades for equalizing income changes to occur.

TRENDS IN WEALTH

In the longer time frame of Figure 6.3, we did not attempt a full cyclical treatment of financial relationships between the valuation ratio q and the real interest rate j as discussed in Chapter 5. Rather, we compressed the observations in earlier chapters into an assumption that capital gains on equity are equal to business profits net of depreciation, taxes, and financial transfers. The vehicle is a price index of equity outstanding, which rises to hold business net worth constant. All profits consequently accrue to households, as in most models of economic growth.

The bulk of capital gains (70 percent) flows to the richest 1 percent. The ratio of equity valuation to business capital is an estimate of q. In panel l, it tends toward a value of 1.2 from an initial level of 0.67 based on Figure 3.6 (in which, it will be recalled, the balance sheets don't balance).

We kept track of wealth for the upper two household groups. Built into the model's accounting, as opposed to Figure 3.6, is the restriction that *total* household wealth equals the value of capital estimated by perpetual inventory plus government debt plus net claims against the rest of the world (negative for the USA). The simulations maintain the assumption that the saving rate of the bottom group is negative. As a consequence, their wealth declines or net debt increases. There is undoubtedly dissipation of poor households' debt (due to default, death, informal or formal bankruptcy, acts of God, etc.), but data are hard to come by. With a dissipation rate of 10 percent, debt of the bottom 60 percent stabilizes at around one-half of GDP.

The wealth/GDP ratio for rich households increases steadily in panel r of Figure 6.3. Government debt and net foreign liabilities do not play significant roles. The corresponding deficits are in the range of a few percent of GDP, with the government's falling and the rest of the world's trending up. The impacts of the mutually offsetting deficits on household wealth accumulation are small. What does matter is the steady increase in q, feeding mostly into wealth of the top 1 percent.

The ratio of their wealth to the total of the top two groups stabilizes in the vicinity of 60 percent (panel s), in line with the Pasinetti accounting discussed in Chapter 5. The simulation model's distribution and saving (really demand leakage) parameters are much more complicated than in the simple theory, but the basic result goes through because the dynamics of q are stable and capital gains fulfills the function of transferring business profits to households. Concentration of wealth in the hands of "capitalists" is held below 100 percent, but the 60 percent ceiling is higher than higher it ever has been in the USA.

WEALTH FUND

As has been emphasized repeatedly, owners of wealth maintain their positions because their large stocks of assets generate high incomes from which their saving rate is high. The macro economy channels their abstinence into ongoing accumulation. A public wealth fund could become an alternative vehicle for accumulation. Perhaps the best-known proposal is still the one put forward in the 1970s by the Swedish trade union economist Rudolf Meidner (1978). Part of the plan involved a fund to be built up from new special shares to be issued by firms, which would support workers' pensions. The fund's accumulation would provide a counterweight to private sector saving. In the recent period, the "oil fund" in Norway (a trillion dollars in assets) and the California public employees' pension fund CalPERS ($300 billion) provide practical examples of well-known publicly controlled institutions.

We can borrow this idea by imposing a tax on capital gains (by assumption equal to net business profits). The proceeds could be transferred to a wealth fund for accumulation. Growing from a zero base, the fund would also receive a share proportional to its size from interest and dividend payments on its investments. Along Meidner's lines, it could transfer a fraction of its assets each year to households with low incomes. The transfer would mimic a guaranteed minimum income, subject over time to asset price fluctuations.

For Meade's reasons noted in Chapter 5, the fund would not take over the economy – rich households have income sources besides finance. Figure 6.6 shows the effects of a fund supported by a 50 percent tax on capital gains combined with a 2 percent transfer of its net worth to the bottom tier of households. The share of rich households in total wealth grows for only a few decades and then starts to taper off, stabilizing at around 0.4 instead of 0.6 (see panel s2). The fund's share steadily increases (panel s3). With lower posttax profits, the valuation ratio q declines after two or three decades (panel 1). Because of its high saving rate (100 percent initially, gradually decreasing over time), an aggressive public fund could make a real dent in the concentration of wealth.

In other results, capital accumulation is led by low income. It speeds up but the overall growth trajectory is not strongly affected (panels a and b). Top-to-bottom Palma ratios are shifted downward (panels p1 and p2).

A REDISTRIBUTIVE PACKAGE

Dynamics of productivity, wages, financial transfers, and proprietors' incomes on one hand and a wealth fund on the other involve processes that are largely independent of each other. Figure 6.7 shows what happens when the redistributive policies illustrated in Figures 6.3 and 6.6 are combined. Income inequality and wealth concentration both go down.

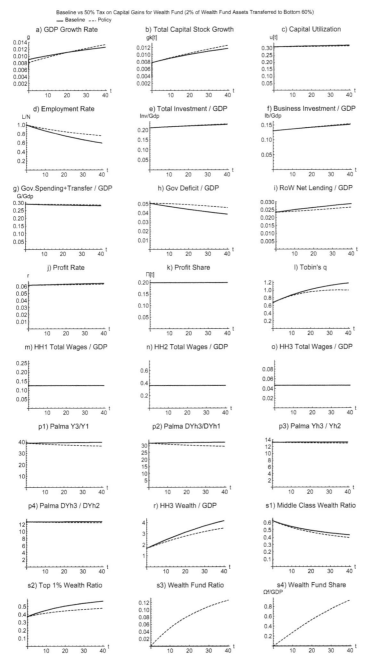

FIGURE 6.6 Tax capital gains by 50 percent to build the wealth fund and transfer 2 percent of wealth fund assets to bottom 60 percent

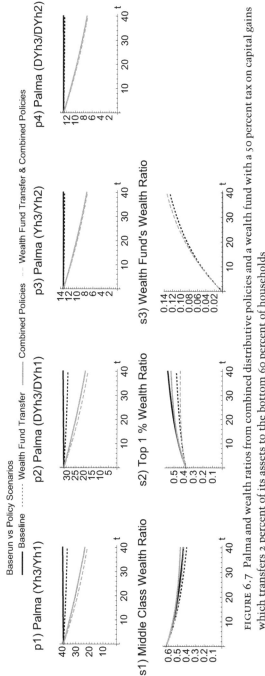

FIGURE 6.7 Palma and wealth ratios from combined distributive policies and a wealth fund with a 50 percent tax on capital gains which transfers 2 percent of its assets to the bottom 60 percent of households

COMPARATIVE STATICS VS. DYNAMICS

The lesson of Figures 6.1 and 6.2 is that one-off policy shifts in the hundred billion dollar range will not affect output and distribution very strongly. The size of an amalgamation of a Green New Deal, free college tuition, and Medicare for all might be around $1 trillion. Likely impacts in a desktop version of the present model (*before* repercussions on inflation and interest rates) could be a $2 trillion increase in GDP, and $450 million and $150 billion in the fiscal and foreign deficits respectively (Taylor, 2019). All numbers are rather large in political terms.

On the other hand, slow and steady growth of real wages at a rate 0.35 percent faster than productivity over four decades together with other redistributive measures and a wealth fund could reverse the observed distributional deterioration since the 1970s. If there is to be an effective double movement, it will have to be cumulative over time.

References

Abraham, Katherine G., John Haltiwanger, Lee Kristin Sandusky, and James Spletzer. (2018). "Measuring the Gig Economy: Current Knowledge and Open Issues," NBER Working Paper No. w24950.

Autor, David H., David Dorn, and Gordon Hanson. (2013). "The China Syndrome: Local Labor Markets Effects of Import Competition in the United States," *American Economic Review, 103* (6): 2121–2168.

Autor, David, H., David Dorn, Lawrence F. Katz, Christina Patterson, and John Van Reenan. (2017). "Superstar Firms and the Falling Labor Share," *American Economic Review: Papers and Proceedings, 107* (5): 180–185.

Barbosa-Filho, Nelson H. (2019). "A Vertical Social Accounting Matrix for the US Economy," *Journal of Post-Keynesian Economics,* forthcoming.

Barbosa-Filho, Nelson H., and Lance Taylor. (2006). "Distributive and Demand Cycles in the U.S. Economy – A Structuralist Goodwin Model, *Metroeconomica, 57:* 389–411.

Baumol, William, and William Bowen. (1966). *Performing Arts: The Economic Dilemma,* New York: Twentieth Century Fund.

Bhaduri, Amit, and Stephen A. Marglin. (1990). "Unemployment and the Real Wage: The Economic Basis for Contesting Political Ideologies," *Cambridge Journal of Economics, 14:* 375–393.

Blanchard, Olivier Jean, and Stanley Fischer. (1989). *Lectures on Macroeconomics,* Cambridge, MA: MIT Press.

Carvalho, Laura, and Armon Rezai. (2016). "Personal Income Inequality and Aggregate Demand," *Cambridge Journal of Economics, 40:* 491–505.

Congressional Budget Office. (2014). "The Effects of a Minimum-Wage Increase on Employment and Family Income," www.cbo.gov/publication/44995.

Congressional Budget Office. (2018). "The Distribution of Household Income, 2014," www.cbo.gov/publication/53597.

Dutt, Amitava Krishna. (1984). "Stagnation, Income Distribution, and Monopoly Power," *Cambridge Journal of Economics, 8:* 25–40.

Dutt, Amitava Krishna. (1990). "Growth, Distribution, and Capital Ownership: Kalecki and Pasinetti Revisited," in Bhaskar Dutta, Shubhashis Gandopadhyay,

Dilip Mookerjee, and Debraj Ray (eds.) *Economic Theory and Policy: Essays in Honour of Dipak Banerjee*, Bombay: Oxford University Press.

Ederer, Stefan, and Miriam Rehm. (2020). "Will wealth become more concentrated in Europe? Evidence from a calibrated Post-Keynesian model," *Cambridge Journal of Economics*, forthcoming.

Eggertsson, Gauti, Jacob A. Robbins, and Ella Getz Wold. (2018). "Kaldor and Piketty's Facts: The Rise of Monopoly Power in the United States," http://020 52018-WP-kaldor-piketty-monopoly-power.pdf.

Fesseau, Maryse, and Peter van de Ven. (2014). "Measuring Inequality in Income and Consumption in a National Accounts Framework," Paris: OECD Statistics Brief No. 19.

Foley, Duncan K., Thomas R. Michl, and Daniele Tavani. (2019). *Growth and Distribution* (2nd edition), Cambridge, MA: Harvard University Press.

Furman, Jason, and Peter Orzag. (2015). "A Firm-Level Perspective on the Role of Rents in the Rise of Inequality," Presentation at "A Just Society" event in honor of Joseph Stiglitz, New York, NY: Columbia University.

Gale, William G., Melissa S. Kearney, and Peter R. Orzag. (2015). "Would a Significant Increase in the Top Income Tax Rate Substantially Alter Income Inequality?" www.brookings.edu/~/media/research/files/papers/2015/09/28-taxes-inequality/would-top-income-tax-alter-income-inequality.pdf.

Glick, Mark. (2019). "Antitrust and Economic History: The Historic Failure of the Chicago School of Antitrust," www.ineteconomics.org/uploads/papers/WP_95-Glick-Antitrust.pdf.

Goodwin, Richard M. (1967). "A Growth Cycle," in C. H. Feinstein (ed.) *Socialism, Capitalism, and Growth*, Cambridge, UK: Cambridge University Press.

Gordon, Myron J. (1959). "Dividends, Earnings, and Stock Prices," *Review of Economics and Statistics*, 41: 99–105.

Harcourt, G. C. (1972). *Some Cambridge Controversies in the Theory of Capital*, Cambridge, UK: Cambridge University Press.

Hicks, John R. (1932). *The Theory of Wages*, London: Macmillan.

Hobsbawm, Eric. (1994). *The Age of Extremes*, New York: Viking.

Houseman, Susan N., Timothy J. Bartik, and Timothy J. Sturgeon. (2014). "Measuring Manufacturing: How the Computer and Semiconductor Industries Affect The Numbers and Perceptions," http://research.upjohn.org/up_workingpapers/209/.

Kaldor, Nicholas. (1978). "Causes of the Slow Rate of Growth of the United Kingdom" in *Further Essays on Economic Theory*, London: Duckworth.

Keynes, John Maynard. (1930). *A Treatise on Money*, London: Macmillan.

Keynes, John Maynard. (1936). *The General Theory of Employment, Interest, and Money*, London: Macmillan.

Keynes, John Maynard. (1940). *How to Pay for the War*. London: Macmillan.

Kiefer, David, and Codrina Rada. (2015). "Profit Maximizing Goes Global: The Race to the Bottom," *Cambridge Journal of Economics, 39*: 1333–1350.

Krueger, Anne. (1974). "The Political Economy of the Rent-Seeking Society," *American Economic Review, 64*: 291–303.

Kuhn, Moritz, Moritz Schularick, and Ulrike I. Steins. (2017). "Wealth and Income Inequality in America, 1949–2013," Bonn, Germany: University of Bonn.

Lazonick, William. (2014). "Profits without Prosperity," *Harvard Business Review*, https://hbr.org/2014/09/profits-without-prosperity.

Lazonick, William. (2015). "Labor in the Twenty-first Century: The Top 0.1% and the Disappearing Middle Class," www.ineteconomics.org/uploads/papers/LA ZONICK.pdf.

Lewis, W. Arthur. (1954). "Economic Development with Unlimited Supplies of Labor," *Manchester School, 22*: 139–19.

McKinnon, Ronald I. (1973). *Money and Capital in Economic Development*, Washington, DC: Brookings Institution.

Meade, J. E. (1964). *Efficiency, Equality, and the Ownership of Property*, London: George Allen & Unwin.

Meidner, Rudolf. (1978 [1976]). *Employee Investment Funds: An Approach to Collective Capital Formation*, London, George Allen & Unwin. [First published in Swedish 1976.]

Mendieta-Muñoz, Ivan, Codrina Rada, and Rudi von Arnim. (2019). *The Decline of the US Labor Share across Sectors*, Salt Lake City: Department of Economics, University of Utah.

Moyer, Brian C., Mark A. Planting, Mahnaz Fahim-Nader, and Sherlene K. S. Lum. (2004). "Preview of the Comprehensive Revision of the Annual Industry Accounts, www.bea.gov/scb/pdf/2004/03March/0304IndustryAcctsV3.pdf.

Palley, Thomas I. (2012). "The Distribution of Wealth: A Missing Variable," *Journal of Post Keynesian Economics, 34*: 449–470.

Palma, José Gabriel. (2009). "The Revenge of the Market on the Rentiers: Why Neo-Liberal Reports of the End of History Turned Out to Be Premature," *Cambridge Journal of Economics, 33*: 829–869.

Pasinetti, Luigi L. (1962). "Income Distribution and Rate of Profit in Relation to the Rate of Economic Growth," *Review of Economic Studies, 29*: 267–279.

Pasinetti, Luigi L. (1974). "The Rate of Profit in an Expanding Economy," in *Growth and Income Distribution: Essays in Economic Theory*, Cambridge: Cambridge University Press.

Piketty, Thomas. (2014). *Capital in the Twenty-First Century*, Cambridge, MA: Belknap Press.

Piketty, Thomas, Emmanuel Saez, and Gabriel Zucman. (2016). "Distributional National Accounts: Methods and Estimates for the United States," NBER Working Paper w22945.

Polanyi, Karl. (1944). *The Great Transformation*, New York: Farrar and Rinehart.

Rada, Codrina. (2007). "A Growth Model for a Two-Sector Economy with Endogenous Employment," *Cambridge Journal of Economics, 31*: 711–740.

Raja, Raghuram, and Luigi Zingalas. (2004). *Saving Capitalism from the Capitalists: Unleashing the Power of Financial Markets to Create Wealth and Spread Opportunity*, Princeton, NJ: Princeton University Press.

Ramsey, Frank P. (1928). "A Mathematical Theory of Saving," *Economic Journal, 38*: 543–559.

Rezai, Armon. (2013). "Cycles of Demand and Distribution and Monetary Policy in the US Economy," *Journal of Post-Keynesian Economics, 36*: 231–250.

Rezai, Armon, Lance Taylor, and Duncan K. Foley. (2018). "Economic Growth, Income Distribution, and Climate Change, *Ecological Economics, 146*: 164–172.

Rowthorn, Robert E. (1982). "Demand, Real Wages, and Economic Growth," *Studi Economici, 18*: 2–53.

Saez, Emmanuel, and Gabriel Zucman. (2015). "Wealth Inequality in the United States since 1913: Evidence from Capitalized Income Tax Data," Berkeley: Department of Economics, University of California.

Samuelson, Paul A. (1966). "A Summing Up," *Quarterly Journal of Economics, 80*: 568–563.

Semieniuk, Gregor. (2018). "Energy in Economic Growth: Is Faster Growth Greener?" *SOAS Department of Economics Working Paper Series*, No. 208, SOAS University of London.

Sen, Amartya. (1966). "Peasants and Dualism with and without Surplus Labor," *Journal of Political Economy, 74*: 425–450.

Shaw, Edward S. (1973). *Financial Deepening in Economic Development*, New York: Oxford University Press.

Solow, Robert M. (1956). "A Contribution to the Theory of Economic Growth," *Quarterly Journal of Economics, 70*: 65–94.

Solow, Robert M. (2015). "The Future of Work: Why Wages Aren't Keeping Up," *Pacific Standard*, August 15, https://psmag.com/the-future-of-work-why-wages-aren-t-keeping-up-6fcfac468e4#.j0iys3wc8.

Sraffa, Piero. (1962). "*Production of Commodities by Means of Commodities*: a comment," *Economic Journal, 72*: 477–479.

Stiglitz, Joseph E. (2016). "Inequality and Economic Growth," in Michael Jacobs and Mariana Mazzucato (eds.), *Rethinking Capitalism: Economics and Policy for Sustainable and Inclusive Growth*, Malden: MA: Wiley-Blackwell.

Stone, J. R. N. (1966). "The Social Accounts from a Consumer Point of View," *Review of Income and Wealth, 12*: 1–33.

Srorm, Servaas. (2017a). "What Mainstream Economists Get Wrong about Secular Stagnation," www.ineteconomics.org/perspectives/blog/what-mainstream-economists-get-wrong-about-secular-stagnation.

Storm, Servaas. (2017b). "The New Normal: Demand, Secular Stagnation, and the Vanishing Middle-Class," www.ineteconomics.org/uploads/papers/WP_55-Storm-The-New-Normal.pdf.

Storm, Servaas, and C. W. M. Naastepad. (2012). *Beyond the NAIRU*, Cambridge, MA: Harvard University Press.

Swan, Trevor W. (1968). "Economic Growth and Capital Accumulation," *Economic Record, 32*: 334–361.

Summers, Lawrence. (2015). "Demand-Side Secular Stagnation," *American Economic Review (Papers and Proceedings), 105* (5): 60–65.

Taylor, Lance. (2017). "The 'Natural' Interest Rate and Secular Stagnation: Loanable Funds Macro Models Don't Fit Today's Institutions or Data," *Challenge, 60*: 27–39.

Taylor, Lance. (2019). "Macroeconomic Stimulus à la MMT," www.ineteconomics.org/perspectives/blog/macroeconomic-stimulus-%C3%A0-la-mmt.

Taylor, Lance, Nelson H. Barbosa-Filho, Codrina Rada von Arnim, and Luca Zamparelli. (2008). "Cycles and Trends in US Net Borrowing Flows," *Journal of Post Keynesian Economics, 30*: 623–647.

Taylor, Lance, Armon Rezai, Rishabh Kumar, Nelson Barbosa, and Laura Carvalho. (2017). "Wage Increases, and the Socially Determined Income Distribution in the USA," *Review of Keynesian Economics, 5*: 259–275.

Taylor, Lance, and Özlem Ömer. (2018a). "Where do Profits and Jobs Come From? Employment and Distribution in the US Economy," www.ineteconomics.org/uploads/papers/WP_72-Taylor-and-Omer-April-8.pdf.

Taylor, Lance, and Özlem Ömer. (2018b). "Market Power, Low Productivity, and Lagging Wages: The Real Drivers," www.ineteconomics.org/perspectives/blog/market-power-low-productivity-and-lagging-wages-the-real-drivers.

Taylor, Lance, Duncan K. Foley, and Armon Rezai. (2019). "Demand Drives Growth All the Way," *Cambridge Journal of Economics, 43*: 1333–1352 .

Temin, Peter. (2015). "The American Dual Economy: Race, Globalization, and the Politics of Exclusion," www.ineteconomics.org/uploads/papers/The-American-Dual-Economy-Race-Globalization-and-the-Politics-of-Exclusion.pdf.

Tobin, James. (1969). "A General Equilibrium Approach to Monetary Theory," *Journal of Money, Credit, and Banking*, 1: 15–29.

Treeck, Till van. (2015). "*r > g*: Why the 'Piketty Debate' Unsettles Germany's Economic Experts," Munich: *CESifo Forum*, 16 (1): 26–34.

Tullock, Gordon. (1967). "The Welfare Costs of Tariffs, Monopoly, and Theft," *Western Economic Journal*, 5: 224–232.

Weil, David. (2014). *The Fissured Workplace*, Cambridge MA: Harvard University Press.

Wolff, Edward N. (2014). "Household Wealth Trends in the United States, 1962–2013: What Happened over the Great Recession?" NBER working paper w20733.

Wu, Tim. (2018). *The Curse of Bigness: Antitrust in the New Gilded Age*, New York: Columbia Global Reports.

Index